*Cover Photo:*
Champagne Bowl 77

Adventures in Cooking SERIES

Illustrations: Karen Rolnick

# COOKING FOR CHRISTMAS

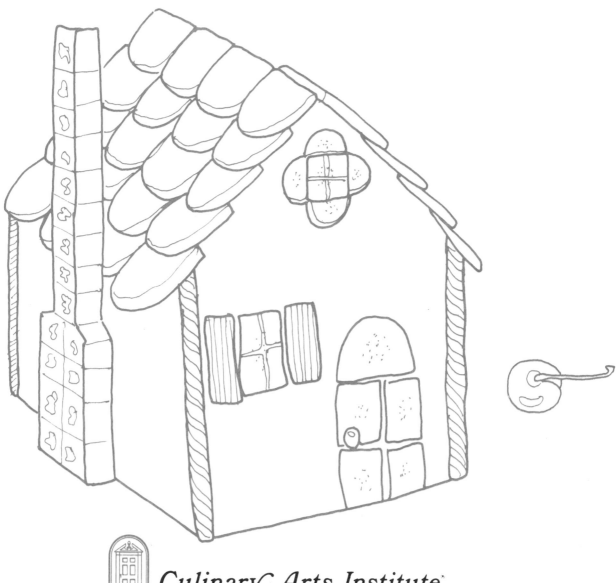

Culinary Arts Institute

A DIVISION OF DELAIR PUBLISHING COMPANY, INC.

ISBN: 0-8326-0640-5

# Contents

# Appetizers

# Clam and Walnut Stuffed Mushrooms

| | |
|---|---|
| **20** | **large mushrooms** |
| ½ | **cup butter or margarine** |
| **1** | **clove garlic, minced** |
| **1** | **can (10 ounces) minced or whole baby clams, drained** |
| **1** | **cup soft bread crumbs** |
| ½ | **cup chopped walnuts** |
| ¼ | **cup chopped parsley** |
| ¼ | **teaspoon salt** |
| ¼ | **teaspoon black pepper** |
| | **Walnut halves (optional)** |
| | **Parsley sprigs (optional)** |

1. Rinse mushrooms and pat dry. Remove stems and chop (about 1 cup); set aside
2. Melt butter in a large skillet. Use about 3 tablespoons of melted butter to brush on mushroom caps. Place caps in a shallow pan.
3. To butter remaining in skillet, add garlic and reserved chopped mushroom stems; saute 2 minutes. Add clams, bread crumbs, nuts, parsley, salt, and pepper; mix well.
4. Spoon stuffing into mushroom caps, piling high.
5. Bake at 350°F about 12 minutes, or until hot.
6. If desired, garnish with walnut halves and parsley sprigs.

*20 stuffed mushrooms*

**Planning Appetizers**

There is no limit to the kinds of meat, poultry, fish, cheese, vegetables, and fruits that can be used. Though imagination and ingenuity are the only limiting factors in selecting appetizers, there is one rule that should be followed—*avoid repeating any food in the main part of the meal that has been used in the appetizers.* Remember that they are a part of the whole menu; select them to harmonize with the rest of the meal. Choose them for complementary flavors, for contrast of texture and color and variety of shape. Picture the serving dishes, trays, and other appointments as you plan the menu.

# Shrimp Cocktail, Seviche Style

1 ½   **lbs. cooked shrimp, shelled, deveined, and chilled**
1   **firm ripe tomato, peeled and diced**
¼   **cup thinly sliced green onions with tops**
¼   **cup thinly sliced celery**
½   **cup lime juice**
1 ½   **teaspoons salt**
3   **teaspoons soy sauce**
¼   **teaspoon Worcestershire sauce**
½   **clove garlic, minced**

1. Dice the chilled shrimp into a bowl and combine with remaining ingredients; toss lightly to mix well. Chill in refrigerator, covered, about 8 hours.
2. Serve very cold on cocktail sea shells lined with leaf lettuce. Or, if desired, spoon cocktail mixture into ripe avocado halves brushed with lime juice.

*6 servings*

# Pimiento-Crab Meat Strata Supreme

1   **can (7½ oz. Alaska King crab meat, drained and flaked**
½   **cup finely chopped celery**
¼   **cup finely chopped onion**
¾   **cup mayonnaise**
  **Few grains cayenne pepper**
12   **slices white bread, crusts removed**
  **Butter or margarine softened**
3   **jars or cans (4 oz. each) whole pimientos, each pimiento cut in 2 or 3 large pieces**
1   **lb. Swiss cheese, shredded**
5   **eggs**
3   **cups milk**
1   **teaspoon salt**
1/8   **teaspoon pepper**
¼   **teaspoon dry mustard**

1. Mix crab meat, celery, and onion. Blend in a mixture of the mayonnaise and cayenne pepper. Set aside.
2. Spread both sides of the bread slices with butter. Place half of the bread in one layer in a greased 3-quart shallow baking dish; reserve remainder.
3. Arrange half of the pimiento pieces over the bread, half of the crab mixture, and a third of the shredded cheese. Repeat layering using remainder of crab mixture, pimiento, and second third of the cheese. Cover with reserved bread and sprinkle with the remaining cheese.
4. Beat remaining ingredients together until frothy and blended. Pour over all. Let stand 1 hour.
5. Bake at 425°F 1 hour, or until puffed and browned.
6. Garnish top with three well-drained whole pimientos arranged in a bell cluster with green pepper strips between the bells. Nestle a small parsley bouquet at center.

*6 to 8 servings*

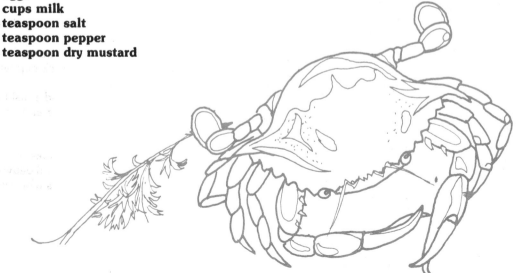

# Avocados Stuffed with Cauliflower Salad

| | |
|---|---|
| 2 | cups very small, crisp raw cauliflowerets |
| 1 | cup cooked green peas |
| ½ | cup sliced ripe olives |
| ¼ | cup chopped pimiento |
| ¼ | cup chopped onion |
| | Oil and Vinegar Dressing (see page 12) |
| | Salt to taste |
| 6 | small lettuce leaves |
| 3 | large ripe avocados |
| | Lemon wedges |

1. Combine all ingredients, except lettuce, avocados, and lemon wedges; stir gently until evenly mixed and coated with dressing.
2. Refrigerate at least 1 hour before serving.
3. When ready to serve, peel, halve, and remove pits from avocados. Place a lettuce leaf on each serving plate; top with avocado half filled with a mound of cauliflower salad. Serve with lemon wedges.

*6 servings*

# Mushrooms a la Grecque

| | |
|---|---|
| 1 | pound fresh mushrooms or 2 cans (6 to 8 ounces each) whole mushrooms |
| ⅓ | cup olive oil |
| ⅓ | cup dry white wine or apple juice |
| ¼ | cup water |
| 1 | tablespoon lemon juice |
| ¾ | cup chopped onion |
| 1 | large clove garlic, minced |
| 1½ | teaspoons salt |
| 1 | teaspoon sugar |
| ½ | teaspoon coriander seed (optional) |
| ¼ | teaspoon black pepper |
| 2 | cups carrot chunks |
| ½ | cup pimento-stuffed olives |

1. Rinse, pat dry, and halve fresh mushrooms or drain canned mushrooms; set aside.
2. In a large saucepan combine oil, wine, water, lemon juice, onion, garlic, salt, sugar, coriander, and black pepper. Bring to boiling; add carrots.
3. Cover and simmer for 15 minutes. Add mushrooms and olives. Return to boiling; reduce heat. Cover and simmer for 5 minutes.
4. Chill thoroughly, at least overnight.
5. To serve, thread mushrooms, carrot chunks, and olives on skewers or spoon into a bowl. Serve as hors d'oeuvres.

*8 to 10 hors d'oeuvre portions*

# Mushroom Cheese Mold

2 packages (8 ounces each) cream cheese, softened
½ pound Cheddar cheese, shredded (about 2 cups)
1 clove garlic, crushed
1½ teaspoons brown mustard
¼ teaspoon salt
1 can (3 to 4 ounces) mushroom stems and pieces, drained and chopped
¼ cup finely chopped onion
2 tablespoons finely diced pimiento
2 tablespoons finely chopped parsley
 Sliced mushrooms (optional)
 Parsley (optional)

1. Combine cheeses, garlic, mustard, and salt in a bowl. Add chopped mushrooms, onion, pimento, and parsley; mix well.
2. Turn mixture into a lightly buttered 3-cup mold. Refrigerate until firm.
3. Unmold onto serving platter. Garnish with sliced mushrooms and parsley, if desired. Serve with **crackers.**

*3½ cups spread*

# Marinated Pimiento Piccante

3 tablespoons red wine vinegar
2 cloves garlic, minced
1 bay leaf
½ teaspoon salt
½ teaspoon pepper
2 tablespoons olive or other cooking oil
2 tablespoons chili sauce
2 jars or cans (7 oz. each) whole pimientos, drained and torn in half or in large pieces
1 can anchovy fillets
¼ cup slivered ripe olives
1 tablespoon lemon juice

1. Put the vinegar, garlic, bay leaf, salt, and pepper into a saucepan; simmer 5 minutes.
2. Blend in oil and chili sauce; pour over pimientos. Let stand about 3 hours.
3. To serve, drain pimientos and garnish with anchovy filets and ripe olives. Drizzle lemon juice over all.

*6 servings*

# Zucchini Vinaigrette

6 medium-sized zucchini
1 pkg. Italian salad dressing mix
¼ cup white wine vinegar
½ cup salad oil
2 tablespoons finely chopped green pepper
2 tablespoons finely chopped parsley
¼ cup finely chopped green onion
3 tablespoons sweet pickle relish

1. Cut ends from each zucchini and slice lengthwise into 6 pieces. Cook in a small amount of boiling salted water about 3 minutes, or until crisp-tender. Drain if necessary and cool; put into a shallow dish.
2. While zucchini is cooling, combine the remaining ingredients in a jar with a tight-fitting lid. Cover and shake vigorously to mix well.
3. Pour vinaigrette sauce over zucchini. Chill 4 hours or overnight. Serve on antipasto tray.

# Soups & Salads

# Chestnut Soup

| | |
|---|---|
| 2 | cups blanched chestnuts |
| 3 | cups water |
| 2 | cups milk, scalded |
| 2 | tablespoons minced onion |
| 4 | tablespoons butter |
| 2 | tablespoons flour |
| 1 | teaspoon salt |
| ¼ | teaspoon pepper |
| 1/8 | teaspoon celery salt |
| | Dash nutmeg |
| 1 | cup cream or evaporated milk |
| | Chopped parsley |

1. To shell and blanch chestnuts: wash and discard those that float. Dry and with a sharp knife make a cross on both sides of the nuts. Place in a baking dish with 1 teaspoon shortening, bake in a hot (450°F.) about 10 minutes.
2. Cool and remove shell and brown skin with knife.
3. Cook chestnuts in water until tender, press through a sieve and add milk. Cook onion in butter until tender, but not brown.
4. Blend in flour, salt, pepper, celery salt and nutmeg. Add milk stirring constantly. Cook 5 minutes, add cream, heat to boiling, garnish with parsley and serve, for 6.

# Poinsettia Salad

| | |
|---|---|
| 1 | No. 2½ can pears |
| ½ | cup red cinnamon drops |
| 3 | tablespoons vinegar |
| 1 | bunch watercress |
| 4 | teaspoons grated sharp Cheddar cheese |
| | Lime French Dressing (page 47) |

1. Combine syrup from pears with cinnamon drops and vinegar and heat to boiling. Cut each pear half into 4 lengthwise slices to represent petals and simmer in syrup for 20 minutes, or until well colored. Chill.
2. Arrange watercress on 4 salad plates. On each arrange 8 petals, clockwise, each curving toward the center to represent a flower.
3. Sprinkle 1 teaspoon grated cheese in center of each flower, and serve with dressing.

*Serves 4*

# Christmas Eve Salad

1 cup diced cooked beets
1 cup diced tart apple, not peeled
1 cup orange sections
1 cup sliced bananas
1 cup diced pineapple (fresh or canned)
Juice of 1 lime
Oil and Vinegar Dressing (see below)
Shredded lettuce
½ cup chopped peanuts
Seeds from 1 pomegranate

1. Drain beets well. Combine beets, apple, oranges, bananas, and pineapple. Refrigerate until ready to serve.
2. Add lime juice to beet-fruit mixture. Add desired amount of dressing and toss until evenly mixed and coated with dressing.
3. To serve, make a bed of shredded lettuce in salad bowl. Mound salad on top. Sprinkle with peanuts and pomegranate seeds.

*8 to 10 servings*

*Oil and Vinegar Dressing:* Mix 2 **tablespoons white wine vinegar, 1½ teaspoons sugar,** and **¼ teaspoon salt.** Add ⅓ **cup salad oil;** mix well.

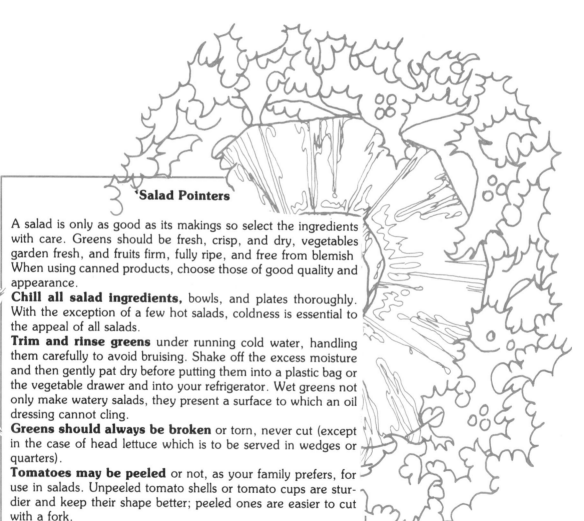

**'Salad Pointers**

A salad is only as good as its makings so select the ingredients with care. Greens should be fresh, crisp, and dry, vegetables garden fresh, and fruits firm, fully ripe, and free from blemish When using canned products, choose those of good quality and appearance.

**Chill all salad ingredients,** bowls, and plates thoroughly. With the exception of a few hot salads, coldness is essential to the appeal of all salads.

**Trim and rinse greens** under running cold water, handling them carefully to avoid bruising. Shake off the excess moisture and then gently pat dry before putting them into a plastic bag or the vegetable drawer and into your refrigerator. Wet greens not only make watery salads, they present a surface to which an oil dressing cannot cling.

**Greens should always be broken** or torn, never cut (except in the case of head lettuce which is to be served in wedges or quarters).

**Tomatoes may be peeled** or not, as your family prefers, for use in salads. Unpeeled tomato shells or tomato cups are sturdier and keep their shape better; peeled ones are easier to cut with a fork.

**Tomato wedges or chunks** should be added to tossed salads just before serving, as their juice tends to make the dressing watery.

# Molded Lobster Elegance

| | |
|---|---|
| 2½ | env. unflavored gelatin |
| 1 | cup cold water |
| 3 | egg yolks |
| 1 | cup strong chicken broth, cooled (dissolve 2 chicken bouillon cubes in 1 cup boiling water) |
| 1¼ | teaspoons salt |
| ¼ | teaspoon pepper |
| 2 | teaspoons grated onion |
| 1 | teaspoon prepared mustard |
| 1 | teaspoon prepared horseradish |
| 3 | cups cooked lobster meat |
| 3 | tablespoons lemon juice |
| 1½ | cups chilled heavy cream, whipped |
| ¼ | cup finely chopped toasted almonds |
| ¼ | cup finely chopped celery |
| ¼ | cup finely chopped pimiento-stuffed olives |

1. Soften the gelatin in the cold water in a small bowl. Set aside.

2. Meanwhile, beat the egg yolks in the top of a double boiler. Add the broth gradually, stirring constantly. Mix in the salt and pepper. Stirring constantly, cook over simmering water until smooth and slightly thickened 5 to 8 minutes.

3. Remove from simmering water, immediately add the softened gelatin, and stir until gelatin is dissolved. Stir in the grated onion, mustard, and horseradish. Cool; chill until mixture is slightly thickened.

4. Cut the lobster meat into small pieces and put into a large bowl. Drizzle lemon juice evenly over lobster.

5. Fold whipped cream into the slightly thickened gelatin mixture. Mix almonds, celery, and olives with the lobster. Pour the whipped cream mixture over lobster and fold together. Turn mixture into a 1½-quart mold. Chill until firm, 4 to 5 hours overnight.

6. Unmold onto a chilled serving plate. Garnish with watercress.

*10 to 12 servings*

# Christmas Wreath Salad

| | |
|---|---|
| 6 | slices pineapple |
| 1 | head romaine Angelica |
| ½ | cup red cinnamon drops Whipped Cream Dressing (page 46) |

1. Arrange 1 slice pineapple on romaine on each plate. Cut angelica to represent holly leaves and arrange on pineapple.

2. Sprinkle cinnamon drops at intervals between the leaves to represent holly. Fill center of pineapple ring with whipped cream dressing.

*Serves 6*

# Almond Soup

| | |
|---|---|
| 5 | cups milk |
| ½ | pound blanched almonds, ground twice |
| 5 | bitter almonds (optional) |
| 1 | teaspoon almond extract |
| 2 | cups cooked rice |
| ⅓ | cup sugar |
| ¼ | cup raisins or currants |

1. Heat milk just to simmering in a large saucepan.

2. Add all the ingredients; stir until well mixed. Cook over low heat 3 to 5 minutes.

3. Serve hot as is traditional for Christmas, or chill before serving.

*About 2 quarts*

# Breads

## Christmas Bread

| | |
|---|---|
| 2 | envelopes active dry yeast |
| 2 | cups scalded milk, cooled to 105° to 115°F |
| 1 | cup sugar |
| 1 | teaspoon salt |
| 4 | eggs (or 8 yolks), well beaten |
| ½ | cup unsalted butter, melted |
| 7½ | to 8 cups all-purpose flour |
| 1½ | teaspoons cardamom, pounded, or 1 teaspoon mastic |
| ½ | cup dried golden currants |
| ¾ | cup chopped walnuts |
| 2 | egg whites, beaten |
| 4 | tablespoons sugar |

1. Sprinkle yeast over 1 cup warm milk in a small bowl; stir until dissolved. Set aside.
2. Reserve 2 teaspoons sugar for pounding with mastic, if using. Put sugar into a bowl and add salt, eggs, remaining 1 cup milk, and butter; mix well.
3. Put 7 cups flour into a large bowl. Stir in cadamon, or pound mastic with 2 tablespoons sugar (so it will not become gummy) and add. Make a well and add dissolved yeast, egg mixture, currants, and nuts; mix well.
4. Knead dough on a floured board, adding the remaining 1 cup flour as required. Knead dough until smooth (5 to 6 minutes).
5. Place dough in a greased bowl. Turn until surface is completely greased. Cover. Set in a warm place until double in bulk.
6. Punch dough down. Form into two round loaves and place in buttered 10-inch pans.
7. Cover and let rise again in a warm place until double in bulk.
8. Bake at 375°F 15 minutes. Remove from oven and brush with beaten egg whites, then sprinkle with sugar. Remove from oven and brush with beaten egg whites, then sprinkle with sugar. Return to oven. Turn oven control to 325°F and bake about 35 to 40 minutes, or until bread is done.

## Kings' Bread Ring

| | |
|---|---|
| 2 | packages active dry yeast or 2 cakes compressed yeast |
| ½ | cup water (hot for dry yeast, lukewarm for compressed) |
| ½ | cup milk, scalded |
| ⅓ | cup sugar |
| ⅓ | cup shortening |
| 2 | teaspoons salt |
| 4 | cups all-purpose flour (about) |
| 3 | eggs, well beaten |
| 2 | cups chopped candied fruits (citron, cherries, and orange peel) |
| | Melted butter or margarine |
| | Confectioners' Sugar Icing |

1. Soften yeast in water.
2. Pour hot milk over sugar, shortening, and salt in large bowl, stirring until sugar is dissolved and shortening melted. Cool to lukewarm. Beat in 1 cup of the flour, then eggs and softened yeast. Add enough more flour to make a stiff dough. Stir in 1½ cups candied fruits, reserving remainder to decorate baked ring.
3. Turn dough onto a floured surface and knead until smooth and satiny. Roll dough under hands into a long rope; shape into a ring, sealing ends together. Transfer to a greased cookie sheet. Push a tiny china doll into dough so it is completely covered. Brush with melted butter.
4. Cover with a towel and let rise in a warm place until double in bulk (about 1½ hours).
5. Bake at 375°F 25 to 30 minutes, or until golden brown.
6. Cool on wire rack. Frost with Confectioners' Sugar Icing and decorate with reserved candied fruit.

*1 large bread ring*

*Confectioners' Sugar Icing:* Blend **1⅓ cups confectioners' sugar, 4 teaspoons water,** and **½ teaspoon vanilla extract.**

## Helpful Hints About Breads

• To glaze tops of fancy breads and rolls brush before baking with slightly beaten egg white mixed with 1 tablespoon milk or water; or egg yolk slightly beaten with a little milk or water.
• To slice newly baked bread, cut with a hot knife.
• To butter bread for thin sandwiches, spread end of loaf with softened butter, then cut off a slice as thin a possible. Repeat buttering and slicing.
• To freshen rolls, place them in a heavy paper bag. Twist top of bag and place in a 400°F oven 10 to 15 minutes. (Or wrap securely in aluminum foil.)
• To prepare crumbs from dry bread, force through the fine blade of food chopper or place dry bread in a small plastic bag and crush with a rolling pin. Crush in an electric blender, if available. If using the food chopper, tie a paper bag onto end of food chopper to keep crumbs from scattering.

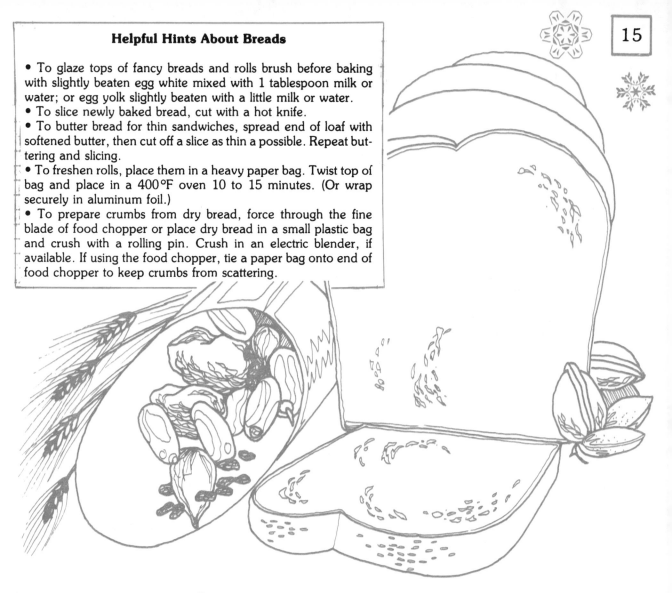

# Norwegian Christmas Bread

| | |
|---|---|
| 1 | cup milk, scalded |
| ½ | cup butter, softened |
| ½ | cup sugar |
| 1 | teaspoon salt |
| 1 | teaspoon ground car-damom |
| 2 | pkgs. active dry yeast |
| ½ | cup warm water |
| ½ | cup currants |
| ½ | cup coarsely chopped almonds |
| ½ | cup mixed candied fruit |
| 1 | tablespoon flour |
| 5 | cups all-purpose flour |
| 1 | egg, beaten |
| 1 | tablespoon sugar |
| ⅛ | teaspoon ground cin-namon |

1. Pour scalded milk over butter, ½ cup sugar, salt, and cardamom in a bowl. Stir until butter is melted. Cool to lukewarm.
2. Soften yeast in the warm water.
3. Toss currants, almonds, and mixed fruit with the 1 tablespoon flour; set aside.
4. Add about 2 cups of the flour to milk mixture and beat until smooth. Stir in yeast, egg and then the fruit-nut mixture. Beat in enough of the remaining flour to make a soft dough.
5. Turn onto a lightly floured surface. Knead dough until smooth and elastic, 5 to 8 minutes. Form into a ball and place in a greased deep bowl. Turn dough to bring greased surface to top. Cover; let rise in a warm place until doubled, about 1½ hours.
6. Punch down dough and turn onto a lightly floured surface. Divide dough into halves and shape each into a round loaf. Place on a greased baking sheet. Cover; let rise again until doubled, about 1 hour.
7. Bake at 350°F 25 minutes. Brush tops with softened butter and sprinkle with a mixture of the sugar and cinnamon. Remove to wire racks to cool.

*2 Loaves Bread*

# Fruit Bread

| | |
|---|---|
| 1 | pound prunes |
| 1 | pound figs |
| 1 | pound dates |
| ¼ | cup raisins |
| ¼ | cup dried currants |
| 1 | tablespoon chopped candied citron |
| 1 | tablespoon chopped candied lemon peel |
| 1 | tablespoon chopped candied orange peel |
| ¼ | cup chopped blanched almonds |
| 2 | cakes yeast |
| 4½ | cups sifted flour |
| ¼ | teaspoon cloves |
| ¼ | teaspoon cinnamon |
| ¼ | teaspoon salt |

1. Soak prunes and figs 1 hour in just enough water to cover.
2. Add dates and cook gently in the same water 20 minutes. Remove fruit, chop and mix with other fruit and nuts.
3. Reduce liquid to ¾ cup. Cool to lukewarm, add yeast and stir until well blended.
4. Add 2 cups flour, beating well. Let rise until light and spongy.
5. Add spices, salt, fruit mixture and remaining flour to make a stiff dough. Knead until smooth. Let rise until doubled in bulk.
6. Shape into oval loaves, brush with slightly sweetened milk and sprinkle with split almonds. Let rise again and bake in hot oven (425°F.) 45 minutes.
7. Makes 3 loaves. If desired, when cool, spread with icing and garnish with candied fruits and nut meats.

# Cranberry Fruit-Nut Bread

| | |
|---|---|
| 2 | cups all-purpose flour |
| 1 | cup sugar |
| 1½ | teaspoons baking powder |
| 1 | teaspoon salt |
| ½ | teaspoon baking soda |
| 1¼ | cups cranberries, cut in halves |
| ½ | cup walnuts, coarsely chopped |
| 1 | egg, well beaten |
| 1 | teaspoon grated orange peel |
| ¾ | cup orange juice |
| 2 | tablespoons melted butter or margarine |

1. Mix flour with sugar, baking powder, salt, and baking soda in a bowl. Mix in cranberries and walnuts.
2. Blend egg, orange peel and juice, and butter in a bowl. Make a well in center of dry ingredients; add liquid mixture and stir only enough to moisten dry ingredients.
3. Turn into a well-greased and floured cooker bake pan or 2-pound coffee can. Cover bake pan with lid; or, if using coffee can, cover with 6 layers of paper toweling. Set in an electric cooker.
4. Cover and cook on High 3 to 4 hours.
5. Remove bake pan and let cool 10 minutes before removing bread.

*1 loaf bread*

# Croustade Basket

| | |
|---|---|
| 1 | loaf unsliced bread |
| ⅓ | cup melted butter or margarine |

1. Neatly trim the crusts from top and sides of loaf. Using a sharp pointed knife, hollow out center, leaving 1-inch sides and bottom.
2. Brush inside and out with melted butter. Place on a baking sheet.
3. Toast in a 400°F oven 10 to 15 minutes, or until golden brown and crisp. Fill with Scrambled Eggs.

# Fish & Shellfish

## Trout in Grapevine Leaves

1 jar (32 ounces) grapevine leaves, drained
4 medium trout, cleaned, with heads and tails left on
2 tablespoons olive oil
2 tablespoons butter, melted
2 teaspoons oregano
1 teaspoon dill
Additional oil to brush outside of trout
Salt and pepper to taste
2 lemons, cut in wedges

1. Rinse grapevine leaves thoroughly under cold running water to remove brine.
2. Rinse trout; pat dry.
3. Drizzle 2 tablespoons olive oil and butter in trout cavities. Sprinkle with oregano and dill. Brush oil on outside of fish. Season inside and out with salt and pepper.
4. Wrap each trout in 5 or 6 grapevine leaves. Refrigerate 1 to 2 hours.
5. To charcoal-broil, adjust grill 4 inches from heated coals. Grease a rectangular, long-handled grill on all sides. Place fish in the grill, side by side. Grill one side about 8 minutes, turn, grill until fish flakes easily with a fork (about 8 minutes more).
6. Discard browned outer leaves. Serve trout in remaining leaves. Garnish with lemon wedges.
*4 servings*

*Note:* Trout may also be broiled under the broiler. For easy turning, use a long-handled grill.

## Fillet of Sole in White Wine

2 pounds sole fillets
½ cup dry white wine
½ cup chopped onion
3 tablespoons butter, melted
2 bay leaves, crushed
1 teaspoon chopped parsley
½ teaspoon salt
¼ teaspoon pepper

1. Put fillets into a greased shallow 2-quart casserole.
2. Mix wine, onion, butter, and dry seasonings. Pour over fish. Cover casserole.
3. Bake at 375°F 25 minutes, or until fish flakes easily when tested with a fork.

*6 servings*

# Cod Sailor Style

2 pounds cod steaks, about 1 inch thick
2 cups canned tomatoes, sieved
¼ cup chopped green olives
2 tablespoons capers
1 tablespoon parsley
1 teaspoon salt
½ teaspoon pepper
½ teaspoon oregano

1. Put cod steaks into a greased 1½-quart casserole.
2. Combine tomatoes, olives, capers, parsley, salt, pepper, and oregano in a saucepan. Bring to boiling and pour over cod.
3. Bake at 350°F 25 to 30 minutes, or until fish flakes easily when tested with a fork.

*4 servings*

# Cooked Shrimp

1 lb. fresh shrimp with shells
2 cups water
3 tablespoons lemon juice
1 tablespoon salt

1. Wash the shrimp in cold water. Drop shrimp into a boiling mixture of remaining ingredients. Cover tightly. Simmer 5 minutes, or only until shrimp are pink in color. (Avoid overcooking as it toughens shrimp.) Drain and cover with cold water to chill. Drain shrimp again.
2. Remove tiny legs from shrimp; peel off shells. Cut a slit along back (curved surface) of each shrimp just deep enough to expose the black vein. With knife point remove vein in one piece. Rinse quickly in running cold water. Drain on absorbent paper. Store in refrigerator until ready to use.

*½ to ¾ Pound Cooked Shrimp*

# Shrimp De Jonghe

1 pound uncooked shrimp
2 tablespoons white wine
  Dash white pepper
2 teaspoons butter
2 slices dried bread or 1 slice bread and 1 slice toast, crumbed
1 clove garlic, diced
2 tablespoons diced leek
1/8 teaspoon salt

1. Clean and rinse uncooked shrimp and arrange in shallow baking dish.
2. Add wine and pepper and dot with butter.
3. Add garlic, leek and salt to crumbs and rub to a smooth paste.
4. Spread on shrimp and bake at 350°F 20 minutes.
5. Serve at once in the baking dish, for 2.

# Fried Scallops

1 cup dry bread crumbs
1 teaspoon salt
½ teaspoon celery salt
1 pound scallops
1 egg
2 tablespoons water

1. Combine crumbs and seasonings.
2. Dip scallops into crumbs, then into egg diluted with water and dip into crumbs again.
3. Saute or fry in hot deep fat (365°F.) 4 to 5 minutes.
4. Serve with Tartare Sauce.

*Serves 4*

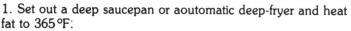
# Deep-Fried Scallops

2 lbs. scallops
1 cup (about 3 slices) fine dry bread crumbs or corn meal
2 eggs, slightly beaten
2 tablespoons milk
2 tablespoons paprika
1 teaspoon salt
¼ teaspoon pepper
Tartar Sauce
Lemon wedges

1. Set out a deep saucepan or aoutomatic deep-fryer and heat fat to 365°F:
2. Set out scallops.
3. (If using frozen scallops, thaw following directions on package.) Rinse scallops in cold water. Set aside to drain on absorbent paper.
4. Put dry bread crumbs or corn meal into a shallow pan or dish and set aside.
5. Mix in bowl eggs, milk, paprika, salt and pepper.
6. Coat scallops, one at a time, by rolling in bread crumbs, dip in egg mixture and then coat again with bread crumbs.
7. Deep-fry in heated fat only as many scallops at one time as will lie uncrowded one layer deep in the fat. Fry 2 or 3 min., or until brown. Turn scallops as they rise to surface and several times during cooking. Remove scallops with a slotted spoon; drain over fat for a few seconds before removing them to absorbent paper.
8. Serve hot with Tartar Sauce and Lemon wedges.

*6 to 8 servings*

*Deep-Fried Oysters:* Follow recipe for Deep-Fried Scallops. Heat fat to 375°F. Substitute **1 qt. large oysters** for the scallops. Drain and pick over to remove any shell particles. (Reserve liquor for use in other food prepartion.)

*Deep-Fried Clams:* Follow recipe for Deep-Fried Scallops. Heat fat to 375°F. Substitute **1 qt. shucked clams** for the scallops.

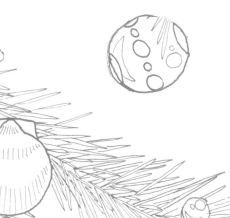

# Deep-Fried Shrimp

Vegetable shortening, all-purpose shortening, lard or cooking oil for deep-frying
2 lbs. fresh shrimp with shells
1 cup (3 slices) fine dry bread crumbs
2 eggs, slightly beaten
2 tablespoons milk
2 tablespoons paprika
1 teaspoon salt
¼ teaspoon pepper
⅛ teaspoon cayenne pepper

1. About 20 min. before ready to deep-fry, fill a deep saucepan or automatic deep fryer one-half to two-thirds full with vegetable shortening, all-purpose shortening, lard or cooking oil for deep-frying.
2. Heat fat slowly to 350°F.
3. Peel shrimp, remove vein and set aside.
4. Put bread crumbs into a shallow pan or dish and set aside.
5. Mix in a bowl eggs, milk, paprika, salt, pepper and cayenne pepper.
6. Dip shrimp into egg mixture and then coat shrimp by rolling in bread crumbs.
7. Deep-fry in the heated fat only as many shrimp at one time as will lie uncrowded one layer deep in the fat. Fry shrimp 2 to 3 min., or until brown. Turn shrimp as they rise to surface and several times during cooking. Remove shrimp with a slotted spoon; drain over fat for a few seconds before removing them to absorbent paper.
8. Serve hot with lemon wedges and melted butter or chili sauce.

*6 to 8 servings*

# Lobster Thermidor I

**3** live lobsters, about 1½ lbs. each
**9** tablespoons butter
**1½** cups Medium White Sauce (one and one half times recipe, page 46; stir into sauce 3 tablespoons heavy cream after removing from heat)
**⅔** cup chopped mushrooms
**2** tablespoons chopped shallots or onion
**3** tablespoons heavy cream
**2** tablespoons white wine
**1** teaspoon finely chopped chervil or parsley
**½** teaspoon Worcestershire sauce
**½** teaspoon dry mustard
**¼** teaspoon salt
**1/8** teaspoon cayenne pepper White wine (about ¼ teaspoon per shell)
**1** egg yolk, slightly beaten
**2** tablespoons whipped cream
**2** tablespoons grated Parmesan cheese

1. Purchase 3 live lobsters
2. Live lobsters may be killed at the market. (Or see Broiled Lobster, page 28). To kill and clean lobster.) Cut completely through shell to divide lobsters into halves; disjoint large and small claws.
3. Heat 6 tablespoons butter in a large heavy skillet with a tight-fitting cover.
4. Add halves of lobster, meat-side down, to skillet. Place large and small claws on top. Cover; cook slowly 12 to 15 min., or until tender. (Lobster meat cooked at a high temperature becomes tough and is difficult to remove from shell.)
5. Meanwhile, prepare medium white sauce.
6. Set aside.
7. Clean and chop mushrooms.
8. Heat 3 tablespoons butter in a saucepan.
9. Add the mushrooms and chopped shallots or onion.
10. Cook over medium heat until mushrooms are tender and lightly browned and onion is soft. Occasionally move and turn mixture with a spoon. Remove from heat.
11. Blend heavy cream, white wine, chevil or parsley, Worcestershire sauce and a mixture of dry mustard, salt and cayenne pepper into one half of the white sauce.
12. Add to the mushroom-onion mixture. Cook over low heat, until thoroughly heated, moving and turning mixture gently with a spoon.
13. When lobster is done, starting at tail, with first and second fingers, gently pry lobster meat from shells, reserving shells. Remove meat from large claws. Place the shells, cavity side up, on a baking sheet and heat at 325°F about 7 min., or until shells are heated.
14. Meanwhile, cut the lobster meat into 1-in. pieces and blend into the sauce.
15. Remove shells from oven and sprinkle white wine over interior of each.
16. Fill the lobster shells with the lobster mixture.
17. Pour remaining white sauce into the top of a double boiler. Stir over low heat until heated. Vigorously stir about 3 tablespoons sauce into egg yolk.
18. Immediately return mixture to top of double boiler. Stirring constantly, cook over simmering water 3 to 5 minutes. Remove from heat and blend in whipped cream.
19. Spoon over lobster mixture in the shells.
20. Set out grated Parmesan cheese.
21. Sprinkle 1 teaspoon of the cheese over each of the filled shells.
22. Place baking sheet on broiler pan with tops of food 2 to 3 in. from heat. Broil 2 to 3 min., or until lightly browned.

*6 servings*

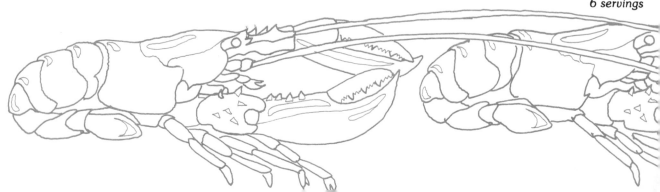

# Lobster Thermidor II

| | |
|---|---|
| **1** | **Boiled Lobster** |
| **3** | **mushrooms, sliced** |
| **¼** | **cup butter** |
| | **Dash paprika** |
| **⅛** | **teaspoon mustard** |
| **1** | **tablespoon minced parsley** |
| **½** | **cup sherry** |
| **1½** | **cups Cream Sauce (page 46)** |
| **2** | **tablespoons grated Parmesan cheese** |

1. Cut lobster lengthwise into halves, remove meat and break it into small pieces.
2. Cook mushrooms 5 minutes in butter; add paprika, mustard, parsley, sherry and 1 cup cream sauce.
3. Mix well, fill lobster shell with mixture, cover with remaining sauce and sprinkle with cheese. Bake in hot oven (450°F.) about 10 minutes.

*Serves 2*

*The cream sauce, may be seasoned more highly if desired. Increase mustard to 1 teaspoon, add 1 teaspoon grated onion and dash celery salt instead of parsley. Increase mushrooms to ¾ cup. Proceed as above.*

# Lobster Tails, Thermidor

| | |
|---|---|
| **2** | **(1½ lbs. each) frozen rock lobster tails** |
| **2** | **tablespoons butter** |
| **2** | **tablespoons flour** |
| **½** | **teaspoon salt** |
| **1** | **teaspoon paprika** |
| **1/8** | **teaspoon Tabasco** |
| **1** | **teaspoon prepared mustard** |
| **1½** | **cups cream** |
| **2** | **cups (½ lb.) shredded Cheddar cheese** |
| **1** | **teaspoon Worcestershire sauce** |
| **¼** | **cup chopped green pepper** |
| **½** | **lb. fresh mushrooms, sliced lengthwise** |

1. Drop frozen lobster tails into boiling salted water. Bring to boiling; simmer 25 to 30 minutes.
2. Meanwhile, heat the 2 tablespoons butter in a large saucepan. Stir in the flour, salt, and paprika and cook until mixture bubbles; blend in Tabasco and mustard. Add cream gradually, stirring until well blended. Bring rapidly to boiling and boil 1 to 2 minutes, stirring constantly. Remove from heat. Add cheese and Worcestershire sauce; stir until cheese is melted. Cover; set aside and keep warm.
3. Remove cooked lobster tails and place under running cold water for 1 minute, or until cool enough to handle. With scissors, cut along each edge of bony membrane on the underside of each shell; remove and discard the membrane.
4. Gently remove meat from shells, cut into ½-inch pieces, and add to sauce. Reserve shells.
5. Heat the ¼ cup butter in a skillet; add green pepper and mushrooms and cook about 5 minutes, or until mushrooms are lightly browned, stirring occasionally. Blend green pepper-mushroom mixture into the cheese sauce.
6. Fill lobster shells with mixture and top with a mixture of **2 tablespoons cracker crumbs, ¼ cup shredded Parmesan cheese,** and **2 tablespoons melted butter.**
7. Set under broiler 4 inches from source of heat 2 to 3 minutes, or until sauce is bubbly and top is lightly browned. Garnish base of each tail with watercress and serve immediately.

*6 servings*

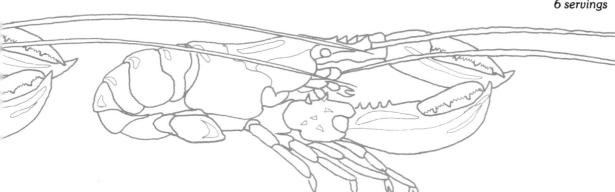

# Fried Clams

| | |
|---|---|
| 1 | quart fresh clams, shucked |
| 2 | eggs, beaten |
| 2 | tablespoons milk |
| 2 | teaspoons salt |
| | Few grains pepper |
| 3 | cups dry bread crumbs |
| | Oil for deep frying |

1. Drain clams and set aside.
2. Combine egg, milk, salt, and pepper. Dip clams in egg mixture and roll in bread crumbs.
3. Heat oil to 350°F in a wok. Fry a few clams at a time in the hot oil 1 to 2 minutes, or until brown. Drain on absorbent paper.
4. Serve hot with tartar sauce.

*About 6 servings*

# Oysters Rockefeller

| | |
|---|---|
| 4 | dozen oysters in half shell |
| | Sauce |
| 8 | slices cooked bacon |
| 2 | cups cooked spinach |
| 3 | tablespoons minced parsley |
| 6 | celery hearts |
| 2 | green onion tops |
| ½ | teaspoon salt |
| ¼ | teaspoon pepper |
| ¼ | teaspoon paprika |
| ½ | cup butter, melted |
| 6 | tablespoons lemon juice |
| 4 | tablespoons cracker crumbs |

1. Heat a 1-inch layer of rock salt in pans and arrange oysters in the half shell over the salt. Broil under moderate heat until edges begin to curl. Prepare sauce: Chop first 5 ingredients very fine.
2. Add remaining ingredients and heat to boiling. Pour hot sauce over each oyster, return pan to oven to brown the sauce slightly and serve at once, serving each guest a panful of oysters.
3. The salt is used to keep the oysters hot and to hold them upright.

*Serve 8*

# Crab Ravigote

| | |
|---|---|
| ¼ | cup butter |
| ¼ | cup flour |
| 1 | teaspoon salt |
| | Few grains cayenne pepper |
| 2 | cups milk |
| ⅔ | cup chopped cooked green pepper |
| ⅔ | cup coarsely chopped pimento |
| 2 | tablespoons capers |
| 2 | teaspoons tarragon vinegar |
| 2 | cups lump crab meat |
| ⅔ | cup Hollandaise Sauce |

1. Heat butter in cooking pan of a chafing dish; blend in flour, salt, and cayenne pepper; heat until bubbly. Gradually add milk, stirring constantly. Cook and stir until boiling; cook 1 minute.
2. Stir in remaining ingredients and heat thoroughly over simmering water.
3. Serve on **rusks.**

*4 servings*

*Hollandaise Sauce:* In the top of a double boiler, beat **2 egg yolks, 2 tablespoons cream, ¼ teaspoon salt** and a **few grains cayenne pepper** until thick with a whisk beater. Set over hot (not boiling) water. Add **2 tablespoons lemon juice or tarragon vinegar** gradually, while beating constantly. Cook, beating constantly with the whisk beater, until sauce is consistency of thick cream. Remove double boiler from heat, leaving top in place. Beating constantly, add ½ **cup butter,** ½ teaspoon at a time, until the butter is melted and thoroughly blended in.

*About 1 cup*

# Vegetables

# Stuffed Artichokes Sicilian

| | |
|---|---|
| 4 | medium artichokes |
| 1 | teaspoon salt |
| ⅔ | cup (2 slices) fine dry bread crumbs |
| 1 | clove plus 3 slices garlic, sliced thin |
| 1 | teaspoon grated Parmesan cheese |
| 1 | tablespoon plus 1 teaspoon chopped parsley |
| 1 | teaspoon salt |
| ¾ | teaspoon pepper |
| 2 | tablespoon olive oil |
| 2 | cups boiling water |

1. Set out a 10-in. dkillet with a tight-fitting cover.
2. Remove outside lower leaves and cut off stems from artichokes.
3. Cover with cold water. Add salt.
4. Let stand 5 to 10 min. Drain upside down.
5. Meanwhile, mix dry bread crumbs, garlic, Parmesan cheese, parsley, salt and pepper.
6. Set aside.
7. Spread leaves of artichokes open slightly and place 3 slices of garlic in each artichoke.
8. Sprinkle crumb mixture between leaves and over top of artichokes. Sprinkle with parsley.
9. Place artichokes close together in skillet so they will remain upright during cooking. Add boiling water.
10. Drizzle artichokes with olive oil.
11. Cover and cook about 30 min., or until artichoke leaves are tender.
12. To eat artichokes, pull out leaves, one by one.

*4 servings*

***Artichokes with Anchovy Dressing:*** Follow recipe for Stuffed Artichokes Sicilian. When preparing artichokes, cut off the top of the leaves and cut out the choke from the center. Discard choke. Add to stuffing **4 anchovy fillets,** chopped. Fill center and between leaves with the stuffing.

# Creamed Peas

**4 cups cooked peas**
**2 cups White Sauce (page 46)**

1. Combine cooked peas with white sauce.
2. Heat in oven or over direct heat.
3. Garnish with sieved hard-cooked egg yolks and sliced hard-cooked egg whites.

*Serves 8*

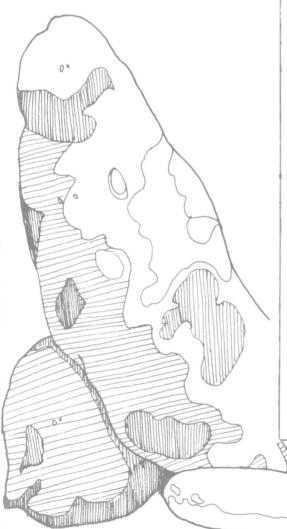

## Helpful Hints About Vegetables

• To freshen fresh asparagus, stand the stalks upright in icy cold water.
• To remove the skins from carrots easily, cover them with boiling water and let stand for a few minutes until the skin loosens.
• To keep cauliflower white while cooking, use half milk and half water; cook, uncovered, until just tender.
• To make celery curls, cut stalks (about 3 inches long) lengthwise into thin strips to within 1 inch of end. Place in cold water until strips begin to curl.
• To make celery very crisp, let stand in icy cold water to which 1 teaspoon sugar per quart of water has been added.
• To garnish lettuce leaves sprinkle some paprika on waxed paper and dip edges of leaves into it.
• To keep onions from affecting eyes, peel them under running water.
• To prevent odor while cooking onions and cabbage, add 1 tablespoon lemon juice or a wedge of lemon to the cooking water.
• To extract juice from onion, cut a slice from the root end and scrape juice from center outward, using edge of a teaspoon.
• To finely cut onion, peel, cut off a slice, then cut exposed surface into 1/8-inch squares as deep as is needed. Then slice across thinly.
• To keep fresh parsley, mint, and watercress fresh and crisp, wash thoroughly, shake off excess water, and place uncrowded in a glass jar; cover and refrigerate.
• To freshen withered parsnips, carrots, potatoes, cabbage, lettuce, etc., let stand in icy cold salted water.
• To keep leftover pimientos from spoiling, put into a small jar, pour enough cooking or salad oil over top to cover, and place, tightly covered, in refrigerator.
• To keep potato skins soft and tender enough to eat, grease them before baking.
• To prevent sweet potatoes and apples from discoloring after paring, place them in salted water at once.
• To remove skin from a tomato quickly, place fork through stem end and plunge tomato into boiling water for a few seconds, then into cold water. Or hold tomato over direct heat for a few seconds; remove from heat and break the skin at blossom end; peel skin back.

# Holiday Onions and Peas

¼ cup flour
1 teaspoon seasoned salt
¼ cup butter or margarine
2 cups milk
24 small white onions (about 1½ lbs.), cooked and drained
1 pkg. (10 oz.) frozen green peas, cooked and drained
2 tablespoons slivered pimiento
1 cup corn flakes
2 tablespoons butter or margarine

1. Blend a mixture of flour and seasoned salt into ¼ cup hot butter in a saucepan. Heat until bubbly. Stir in the milk and bring to boiling; cook and stir 1 to 2 minutes.
2. Mix onions, peas, and pimiento into sauce. Turn mixture into 1½-quart baking dish.
3. Coat corn flakes with 2 tablespoons hot butter in a skillet. Top creamed mixture with buttered corn flakes.
4. Heat in a 350°F oven until mixture is hot and bubbly, about 25 minutes.

*About 8 servings*

# Asparagus Supreme

2 tablespoons minced onion
2 tablespoons butter or margarine
1 tablespoon flour
½ teaspoon salt
½ teaspoon paprika
¼ teaspoon dry mustard
½ teaspoon Worcestershire sauce
1 cup undiluted evaporated milk
3 pkgs. (10 oz. each) frozen asparagus pieces cooked and drained
4 oz. process sharp Cheddar cheese, shredded
2 tablespoons fine dry bread crumbs

1. Cook onion in hot butter in a saucepan until onion is soft, but not browned. Blend in flour, salt, paprika, dry mustard, and Worcestershire sauce. Heat until bubbly.
2. Remove from heat. Add the evaporated milk gradually, stirring constantly. Bring to boiling; cook 1 to 2 minutes.
3. Turn asparagus into a 1-quart shallow baking dish. Pour sauce over asparagus and mix lightly with a fork. Sprinkle the cheese and bread crumbs over top.
4. Set under broiler with top of mixture 2 to 3 inches from source of heat and broil 3 to 5 minutes, or until crumbs are lightly browned and cheese is melted.

*About 8 servings*

# Broiled Mushrooms

12 large mushrooms
2 tablespoons butter
¼ teaspoon salt
1/8 teaspoon pepper

1. Scrub mushrooms and remove stems. Place caps on greased broiler rack, cap side down, about 3 inches below source of heat.
2. Broil 3 minutes, then turn over and broil 3 minutes longer. Put a piece of butter in each cap, sprinkle with salt and pepper and broil until butter melts.
3. Serve on buttered toast.

*Serves 6*

# Artichokes in Mushroom Cream

| | |
|---|---|
| 2 | packages (9 ounces each) frozen artichoke hearts |
| ¼ | cup butter |
| 4 | ounces mushrooms, coarsely chopped |
| 2 | tablespoons finely chopped onion |
| 2½ | tablespoons flour |
| ¼ | teaspoon salt |
| ⅛ | teaspoon white pepper |
| ⅛ | teaspoon ground nutmeg |
| ¾ | cup chicken broth (dissolve 1 chicken bouillon cube in ¾ cup boiling water) |
| ¾ | cup cream |
| 2 | egg yolks, slightly beaten |
| 2 | tablespoons snipped parsley |
| ½ | teaspoon capers |
| 8 | patty shells |

1. Cook artichoke hearts according to package directions, substituting **seasoned salt** for salt. Drain and set aside.

2. Meanwhile, heat butter in cooking pan of a chafing dish; add mushrooms and onion. Cook, stirring occasionally, until mushrooms are lightly browned.

3. Blend in a mixture of the flour, salt, pepper, and nutmeg. Heat until bubbly. Remove from heat and add broth and cream gradually, stirring constantly; bring sauce to boiling and cook 1 to 2 minutes, stirring constantly.

4. Remove from heat and vigorously stir about 3 tablespoons of the mixture into egg yolks. Immediately return to double boiler. Cook over boiling water about 5 minutes, stirring slowly so mixture cooks evenly.

5. Mix in artichoke hearts, parsley, and capers. Heat thoroughly over simmering water.

6. Spoon mixture into warm patty shells. Replace patty shell tops or garnish with tiny fancy shapes cut from a crimson **cinnamon apple** or a **grenadine pear**.

*8 servings*

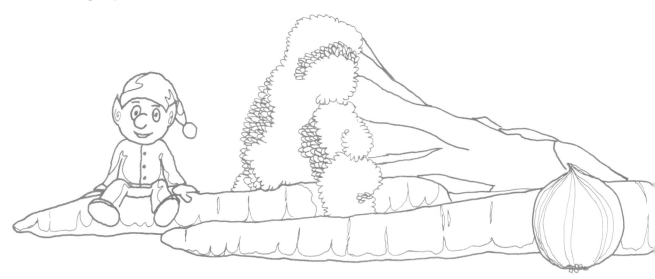

# Creamed Mushrooms

| | |
|---|---|
| 1 | pound mushrooms |
| 5 | tablespoons butter |
| ½ | teaspoon salt |
| ⅛ | teaspoon pepper |
| 2 | tablespoons flour |
| 1½ | cups milk |

1. Cut off all but ½ inch of mushroom stems.
2. Wash mushrooms thoroughly, dry and slice.
3. Cook mushrooms in butter until nearly tender; add salt, pepper and flour and mix well.
4. Add milk gradually and simmer 5 to 8 minutes, stirring constantly.

*Serves 6 to 8*

# Sauteed Mushrooms

| | |
|---|---|
| 1 | pound mushrooms |
| 3 | tablespoons butter |
| ½ | teaspoon salt |
| | Dash pepper |

1. Cut off all but ½ inch of mushroom stems.
2. Wash mushrooms thoroughly, leave whole or slice and cook, covered, in butter 10 to 15 minutes.
3. Season with salt and pepper.

*Serves 6 to 8*

# Cooked Broccoli

| | |
|---|---|
| 2½ | pounds broccoli |
| | Boiling water |
| 1 | teaspoon salt |

1. Wash broccoli and split thick heads. Place broccoli in boiling salted water, with ends down and heads out of water. Cook uncovered 10 to 20 minutes. Then place all of broccoli under water and cook 5 minutes longer. Drain (makes about 4 cups).
2. To serve, season with pepper and butter.

*Serves 6 to 8*

*With White Sauce* — Combine with 1 cup White Sauce (page 46).

*With Hollandaise Sauce* — Serve cooked broccoli with 1 recipe Hollandaise Sauce (page 22).

# Cauliflower Supreme

| | |
|---|---|
| ½ | lb. fresh mushrooms sliced |
| ½ | cup butter |
| ½ | cup all-purpose flour |
| 1 | teaspoon salt |
| 2 | cups milk |
| 2 | pkgs. (10 oz. each) frozen cauliflower, cooked and drained |
| 6 | slices pasteurized process pimiento, cheese and Paprika |

1. Cook mushrooms in hot butter in a skillet until lightly browned. Remove mushrooms with slotted spoon and set aside.
2. Blend flour and salt into butter in skillet. Heat until bubbly. Add milk gradually, stirring constantly. Continue stirring and bring rapidly to boiling; cook 1 to 2 minutes. Stir in mushrooms.
3. Arrange half of cauliflower over bottom of lightly greased 1½-quart casserole. Cover with half of the sauce and 3 slices of cheese. Repeat layering. Sprinkle top with paprika.
4. Heat in 350 °F oven about 15 minutes, or until cheese is melted and mixture is bubbly.

*6 to 8 servings*

# Brussels Sprouts with Chestnuts

½ lb. Brussels sprouts
1 beef bouillon cube
½ lb. chestnuts
½ teaspoon salt
Few grains pepper
Few grains ground nutmeg
Butter or margarine
¼ cup buttered bread crumbs

1. Cook Brussels sprouts; drain, reserving ½ cup liquid. Dissolve bouillon cube in liquid; set aside.
2. Rinse chestnuts, make a slit on two sides of each shell and put into a saucepan; cover with boiling water and boil about 20 minutes.
3. Remove shells and skins; return nuts to saucepan and cover with boiling salted water. Cover and simmer 8 to 20 mintues or until chestnut are tender; drain.
4. Mix chestnuts with Brussels sprouts. Turn one half of mixture into a buttered 1-quart casserole. Sprinkle with half of a mixture of salt, pepper, and nutmeg. Dot generously with butter. Repeat procedure. Pour beef broth over all. Sprinkle with buttered crumbs.
5. Heat in 350°F oven 15 to 20 minutes, or until crumbs are lightly browned.

*4 servings*

# Sauerkraut with Dried Peas (for Christmas Eve)

1 cup dried split green or yellow peas, rinsed
2⅔ cups boiling water
1 quart sauerkraut, rinsed and drained
½ cup chopped mushrooms
3 cups water
Salt and pepper
1 can (2 ounces) anchovies, drained

1. Combine peas and 2⅔ cups boiling water in a saucepan. Bring to boiling and boil 2 minutes. Remove from heat. Cover and let soak 30 minutes. Bring to boiling; simmer 20 minutes.
2. Cover sauerkraut and mushrooms with 3 cups water in a saucepan; cover and cook 1 hour.
3. Add cooked peas to sauerkraut mixture. Season to taste with salt and pepper; mix well. Turn into a buttered baking dish. Top with anchovies. Cover.
4. Bake at 325°F 30 minutes.

*4 to 6 servings*

*Sauerkraut with Dried Peas*: Prepare Sauerkraut with Dried Peas; omit anchovies and baking. Fry **1 onion, chopped,** with ½ **pound salt pork or bacon,** chopped, until lightly browned. Blend in **2 tablespoons flour** and add **1 cup sauerkraut cooking liquid.** Cook and stir until smooth. Mix with sauerkraut and peas; heat thoroughly.

# Boiled New Potatoes

1½ pounds small new potatoes
¼ cup butter, melted
Salt and pepper to season

1. Wash potatoes and cook with jackets on in boiling salted water to cover until tender, 15 to 20 minutes.
2. Peel. Pour butter over potatoes and season with salt and pepper. Juice of ½ lemon may be added to butter.

*For 6*

*Parsley* — Roll boiled potatoes in ½ cup chopped parsley.

# Stuffed Potatoes

| | |
|---|---|
| 6 | medium-sized baking potatoes, baked |
| ½ | cup coarsely chopped onion |
| ½ | cup coarsely chopped green pepper |
| 3 | tablespoons butter or margarine |
| 1 | medium-sized tomato, chopped |
| 2 | tablespoons milk |
| 2 | tablespoons butter or margarine |
| 2 | teaspoons salt |
| ¼ | teaspoon white pepper |
| 1 | teaspoon paprika |
| ¼ | teaspoon crushed rosemary leaves |

1. While potatoes are baking, cook onion and green pepper in 3 tablespoons hot butter in a skillet. Add tomato and cook 1 minute.

2. Cut a thin lengthwise slice from each baked potato. With a spoon, scoop out each potato without breaking skin. Thoroughly mash or rice scooped-out potato. Whip in milk with remaining ingredients until potatoes are fluffy, Blend in vegetable mixture.

3. Pile mixture lightly into potato shells. Arrange on baking sheet. Sprinkle with paprika.

4. Bake at 400°F 20 minutes, or until thoroughly heated and lightly browned.

*6 servings*

# Boiled Sweet Potatoes

Sweetpotatoes
Boiling water
Salt

1. Sweet potatoes and yams are usually cooked with skins on.
2. Wash and rinse; cover with boiling salted water and cook until tender, 20 to 30 minutes.
3. Drain, peel and serve piping hot. Allow 1 medium potato to a serving.

# Sweet Potatoes With Applesauce

| | |
|---|---|
| 3 | large sweet potatoes |
| ¼ | cup butter |
| ¼ | cup brown sugar |
| 2 | cups thick Applesauce |

1. Pare sweet potatoes and cut into 1-inch cubes.
2. Cook for 15 minutes in rapidly boiling water.
3. Place sweetpotatoes in greased baking dish, dot with butter and brown sugar. Pour applesauce over potatoes.
4. Bake in moderate oven (350°F) until tender, about 30 minutes.

*Serves 6*

# Sweet Potato Casserole

| | |
|---|---|
| 6 | sweet potatoes, cooked and sliced |
| ½ | cup brown sugar |
| 5 | tablespoons butter |
| 2 | oranges |
| ½ | cup orange juice |
| ¼ | cup strained honey |
| ¼ | cup fine bread crumbs |

1. In greased casserole, arrange a layer of sliced sweetpotatoes, sprinkle with 6 tablespoons brown sugar, dot with 4 tablespoons butter and cover with a layer of thinly sliced. unpeeled oranges.Repeat layers. Over all, pour orange juice with which honey has been mixed.
2. Combine bread crumbs with remaining 2 tablespoons brown sugar and 1 tablespoon butter and sprinkle over top. Cover casserole and bake in moderate oven (350°F.) 30 to 40 minutes, removing cover last 15 minutes.

# Marshmallow Sweet Potatoes

| | |
|---|---|
| 8 | medium sweet potatoes |
| 2 | tablespoons butter |
| ½ | cup hot milk |
| ½ | teaspoon salt |
| 1 | teaspoon cinnamon or nutmeg |
| ¼ | teaspoon paprika |
| 1 | cup choppe walnuts |
| ½ | pound marshmallows |

1. Cook sweet potatoes until tender, remove skins and mash.
2. Add butter, milk, salt, cinnamon or nutmeg and paprika.
3. Beat until free from lumps and light and fluffy. Fold in walnuts.
4. Turn into a greased casserole, cover with marshmallows and bake in a moderate oven (350°F.) until mixture is heated through and marshmallows are brown.

*Serves 8*

# Mashed Sweet Potatoes

| | |
|---|---|
| 6 | medium boiled sweet potatoes |
| 3 | tablespoons butter |
| ⅓ | cup hot milk |

1. Combine ingredients and beat until light and fluffy. It may be necessary to add more milk if potatoes are dry. Makes 4 cups mashed sweet potatoes.
2. Add dash of nutmeg.
3. Form mashed sweet potatoes into balls with a half with a half or a whole marshmallow in center of each.
4. Roll in shredded coconut and bake in a moderate oven (350°F.) until heated through and a delicate brown.
5. Form balls of mashed sweet potatoes and roll in crushed cereal flakes. Brown in the oven.
6. One or 2 eggs or egg whites, beaten, may be added to mashed sweet potatoes·before shaping into balls and baking.

*Serves 6*

# Sweet Potatoes in Orange Cups

2 cups mashed sweet potatoes
2 tablespoons butter
½ teaspoon salt
½ cup orange juice
3 large oranges
6 marshmallows, quartered

1. Combine sweet potatoes, butter, salt and orange juice. Mix well.
2. Cut oranges in halves, crosswise, and remove juice and pulp (use part of this juice, when mashing potatoes).
3. Scrub shells well.
4. Fill with the mashed potatoes and decorate with marshmallows.
5. Bake in hot oven (400°F.) about 15 minutes.

*Serves 6*

*Sweet Potato Pie —* Omit oranges and marshmallows. Increase butter to ⅓ cup, add 1 cup sugar, 4 eggs, beaten, 1 cup milk, 1 teaspoon cinnamon, ½ teaspoon nutmeg and 1 teaspoon grated orange rind. Mix well and bake in 2 pastry lined pans at 350°F. until firm.

# Scalloped Sweet Potatoes and Apples

6 medium sweet potatoes, pared and cut in crosswise slices ¼ inch thick
1½ cups apple slices
½ cup firmly packed brown sugar
¼ cup butter or margarine, melted
½ cup apple juice
1 tablespoon lemon juice

1. Combine ingredients in an electric cooker.
2. Cover and cook on High 3 to 4 hours, or until sweet potatoes and apples are tender.

*About 6 servings*

# Elegant Apricot Sweet Potatoes

½ lb. (1½ cups) dried apricots
2 cups water
6 medium (about 2 lbs.) sweet potatoes or yams
1 cup firmly packed dark brown sugar
3 tablespoons melted butter
1 teaspoon grated orange peel
2 teaspoons orange juice
¼ cup (about 1 oz.) pecan halves

1. A shallow 1-qt. baking dish will be needed.
2. Put dried apricots into a heavy saucepan.
3. Add water.
4. Bring water to boiling, reduce heat, and cook, covered, about 25 min., or until apricots are plump and tender when pierced with a fork. (Be careful not to overcook the fruit.) Remove saucepan from heat. Cool and drain well, reserving liquid.
5. Meanwhile, wash and scrub with a vegetable brush sweet potatoes or yams.
6. Cook 30 to 35 min., or until potatoes are tender when pierced with a fork. Drain potatoes and peel; cut into lengthwise slices about ½ in. thick.
7. Lightly grease the baking dish.
8. Set out brown sugar.
9. Arrange a layer of the sweet potatoes in the baking dish. Cover with a layer of apricots. Sprinkle with one half of the brown sugar. Repeat layers of sweet potaotes and apricots and sprinkle with remaining sugar.
10. Blend thoroughly ¼ cup of the reserved apricot liquid and melted butter, orange peel and orange juice.
11. Pour mixture over the layers.
12. Bake at 375°F 30 to 45 min., basting occasionally with liquid in bottom of baking dish. About 5 min. before sweet potatoes are done. Top with pecan halves.

*6 to 8 servings.*

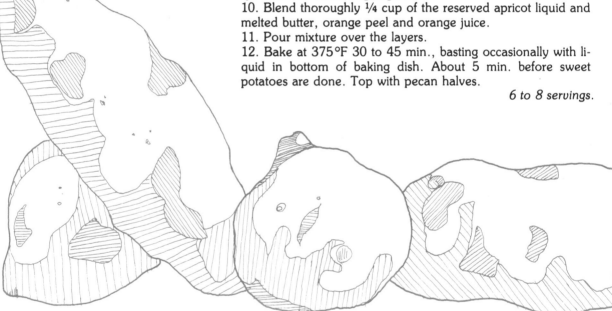

# Orange Candied Sweet Potatoes

6 medium sweet potatoes
1 cup orange juice
½ teaspoon grated orange rind
1 cup water
1 sugar
¼ cup butter
½ teaspoon salt

1. Pare potatoes, slice in ¼-inch slices and arrange in a greased baking dish.
2. Combine remaining ingredients, heat to boiling, and boil until sugar is dissolved; pour over the potatoes. Cover and bake in moderate oven (350°F) until tender, about 45 to 60 minutes.
3. Baste occasionally. Uncover to brown during the last 10 minutes. If desired, a layer of marshmallows may be added and browned just before removing from the oven.

*Serves 6*

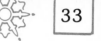

# Cooked Turnips or Rutabagas

| | |
|---|---|
| 2½ | pounds turnips |
| 1 | cup water |
| 1 | teaspoon salt |

1. Pare turnips and cut into cubes.
2. Heat water and salt to boiling, add turnips, cover pan tightly to prevent escape of steam and heat again to boiling.
3. Reduce heat at once and simmer 20 to 35 minutes. Drain if necessary. (Makes about 4 cups, mashed.)
4. To serve, season with pepper and melted butter.
5. To prepare milder-flavored vegetable, cook as for Cooked Cabbage, being very careful not to overcook the turnips.
6. Diced young white turnips will cook tender in 15 to 20 minutes.

*Serves 6 to 8*

# Mashed Turnips

| | |
|---|---|
| 4 | cups Cooked Turnips |
| ⅛ | teaspoon pepper |
| 3 | tablespoons butter |

Mash turnips and add pepper and butter. Beat over low heat until smooth and most of liquid has evaporated.

*Serves 6 to 8*

# Honey-Glazed Turnips

| | |
|---|---|
| 6 | white turnips |
| 1 | cup chicken broth |
| 3 | tablespoons honey |
| ¼ | teaspoon salt |
| ¼ | teaspoon white pepper |
| | Paprika |

1. Pare and slice turnips.
2. Bring broth to a boil in a large saucepan. Add turnips; boil covered, 5 minutes. Remove cover and continue cooking over low heat until most of liquid has evaporated.
3. Add honey, salt, and pepper. Put into a 1½-quart casserole. Cover and refrigerate overnight.
4. Bake, covered, at 350°F 30 minutes, or until heated through. If desired, sprinkle with snipped parsley.

*6 servings*

# Glazed Onions

| | |
|---|---|
| 4 | tablespoons melted butter |
| 3 | tablespoons lemon juice |
| 6 | tablespoons honey |
| 3½ | cups Cooked Onions |

1. Combine first 3 ingredients, add cooked onions and heat slowly 8 minutes or until onions are glazed.

*Serves 6 to 8*

Meat-Stuffed Manicotti  42

# Meat & Poultry

## Baked Ham

**1  smoked ham**
**Glaze, Whole cloves**

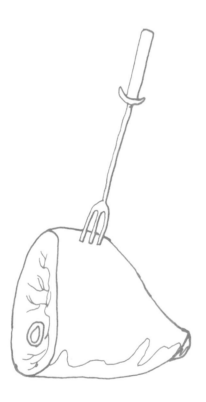

Have ham warmed to room temperature and bake according to directions given by packer, or as follows.

1. Wipe ham with clean cloth, wrap loosely in one of the papers wrapped around ham or in clean wrapping paper and place fat side up on rack of shallow pan.

2. Do not cover pan or add water. For baking allow allow 15 minutes per pound for hams, 12 pounds or over; allow 18 minutes per pound for hams, under 12 pounds; allow 22 minutes per pound for half hams; or bake to an internal temperature of 150°F., being sure bulb of thermometer is inserted into center of thickest part of meat and does not touch bone.

3. Bake in slow oven (325°F.) until within 45 minutes of total baking time. Remove paper and rind from ham, make a series of shallow cuts across fat to cut into squares or diamonds, spread with desired glaze and insert 1 clove into each square of fat. Bake uncovered in 325°F oven for remaining 45 minutes.

### Glazes:

One cup brown sugar, juice and grated rind of 1 orange.
One cup brown or white sugar and ½ cup maraschino cherry juice, cider or sweet pickle juice from pickled fruit.
One cup honey.
One cup brown sugar, 1 tablespoon mustard.
One cup pureed apricots, rhubarb or applesauce.
One glass currant jelly, melted. Use maraschino cherries and mint cherries fastened with pieces of toothpicks instead of cloves.
Three-fourths cup pineapple juice, ¾ cup strained honey and ½ teaspoon mustard cooked until thick.
One-half cup orange marmalade.
Cook ½ pound fresh cranberries with 1 cup maple syrup until skins pop open. Press mixture through sieve and spread over ham.

*Decorate baked ham with golden stars of orange peel to give dinner an extra sparkle.*

# How to Carve

## Whole Ham

1. Ham is placed on platter with decorated or fat side up and shank to carver's right. Location of bones in right and left hams may be confusing so double check location of knee cap which may be on near or far side of ham. Remove two or three lengthwise slices from thin side of ham which contains knee cap.

2. Make perpendicular slices down to leg bone.

3. Release slices by cutting along leg bone.

## Poultry

**Standard Style**

1. To remove leg (drumstick and thigh), hold the drumstick firmly with fingers, pulling gently away from body of bird. At the same time cut through skin between leg and body.

2. Press leg away from body with flat side of knife. Then cut through joint joining leg to backbone and skin on the back. Hold leg on service plate with drumstick at a convenient angle to plate. Separate drumstick and thigh by cutting down through the joint to the plate.

3. Slice drumstick meat. Hold drumstick upright at a convenient angle to plate and cut down, turning drumstick to get uniform slices. Drumsticks and thighs from smaller birds are usually served whole.

4. Slice thigh meat. Hold thigh firmly on plate with a fork. Cut slices of meat parallel to the bone.

5. Cut into white meat parallel to wing. Make a cut deep into the breast to the body frame parallel to and close to the wing.

6. Slice white meat. Beginning at front, starting halfway up the breast, cut thin slices of white meat down to the cut made parallel to the wing. The slices will fall away from the bird as they are cut to this line. Continue carving until enough meat has been carved for first servings. Carve more as needed.

**Side Style**

1. Remove wing tip and first joint. Grasp wing tip firmly with fingers, lift up, and cut between first and second joint. Place wing tip and first joint portion on side of platter. Leave second joint attached to bird.

2. Remove the drumstick. Grasp end of drumstick and lift it up and away from the body, disjointing it from the thigh. Thigh is left attached to the bird. Place drumstick on service plate for slicing. Hold drumstick upright at an angle and cut down toward plate, parallel with bone, turning to make even slices.

3. Anchoring the fork where it is most convenient to steady the bird, cut slices of thigh meat parallel to the body until the bone is reached. Run the point of the knife around the thigh bone, lift up with fork, and remove bone. Slice the remaining thigh meat.

4. Begin at front end of bird and slice white meat until the wing socket is exposed. Remove second joint of wing. Continue slicing until enough slices have been provided, or until the breastbone is reached.

5. Remove stuffing from hole cut into cavity under thigh. Slit the thin tissue in the thigh region with tip of knife and make an opening large enough for a serving spoon. Stuffing in breast cavity may be served by laying the skin back.

# Savory Roast Ham

| | |
|---|---|
| 10 | lb. smoked whole ham |
| 1 | cup firmly packed brown sugar |
| 1 | tablespoon all-purpose flour |
| 1 | teaspoon dry mustard |
| 2 | tablespoons cider vinegar |
| 1 | can (8 ¼ oz.) pineapple tidbits (about ⅔ cup, drained) |
| 1 | orange |
| 8 | maraschino cherries |
| 1 | can (20 oz.) pineapple slices |
| | Melted butter or margarine |
| | Brown sugar |
| | Sprigs of parsley |

1. For Ham—Set out a shallow roasting pan with a rack.
Follow directions on wrapper for roasting or roast as directed below.
Place ham fat side up on rack. Insert roast meat thermometer in thickest part of lean, being sure bulb does not rest on bone or in fat.
Roast uncovered at 300°F 2½ hrs.
Meanwhile, prepare Glaze and Fruit Garnish.

2. For Glaze and Fruit Garnish—Mix in a small bowl brown sugar, all purpose flour, and dry mustard.
Add and stir in cider vinegar to form a smooth paste. Set aside.
Drain (reserving syrup for use in other food preparation) pineapple tidbits and set aside.
Rinse orange.
With a sharp knife, cut away peel through colored part only (white is bitter). Cut peel into desired shapes for decorating; set aside.
Thoroughly drain maraschino cherries.
Cut two cherries into thin slices and remainder into halves. Set aside.

3. To Glaze and Garnish Ham—Remove ham from oven after it has roasted 2½ hrs. Remove rind (if any), being careful not to remove fat. Making diagonal cuts, score fat surface of ham to make diamond pattern; or use scalloped cookie cutter to make flower pattern. Spread about one half of Glaze over ham. Arrange pineapple tidbits, whole and sliced maraschino cherries, and pieces of orange peel on ham in an attractive design, and press firmly into glaze. Carefully spread remainder of Glaze over fruit. Return ham to oven and continue roasting about 45 min., or until internal temperature of ham reaches 160°F. (The total roasting time is about 3 hrs., allowing 18 to 20 min. per pound.) Remove ham from oven; remove thermometer. Keep ham hot. Allow to stand 15 to 20 min. before serving. This helps to make meat easier to carve.

4. For Pineapple Garnish—Drain pineapple slices, reserving syrup for use in other food preparation.
Place slices on broiler rack or a baking sheet. Brush tops with butter or margarine.
Sprinkle with brown sugar.
Place under broiler with tops of pineapple slices 3 in. from heat. Broil 5 to 6 min., or until brown sugar is melted and pineapple slices are lightly browned.
Garnish ham platter with the pineapple and sprigs of parsley.

*About 20 servings*

*Savory Roast Half Ham:* Follow recipe for Savory Roast Ham. Substitute **5-lb. smoked half ham** for the whole ham. Allow 22 to 25 min. per pound for roasting. Prepare and apply one half of the Glaze and Fruit Garnish.

*About 10 servings*

# Butter-Roasted Turkey

*These instructions for roasting make use of an aluminum-foil tent.*

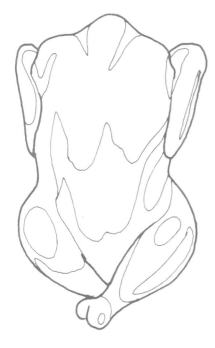

1. Rinse a ready-to-cook turkey, drain, and pat dry. Rub the body and neck cavities with salt. Fill lightly with desired stuffing. (Extra stuffing may be put into a greased covered baking dish or wrapped in aluminum foil and baked with turkey the last hour of roasting time.) Fasten neck skin to back with skewer and bring wing tips onto back. Push drumsticks under band of skin at tail, or tie with cord.
2. Place turkey, breast down, on foil band* put crosswise onto a rack in a foil-lined roasting pan. Brush turkey with softened butter. Roast at 325°F.
3. When turkey has roasted for about two-thirds the required time, remove from oven. Use the boil band to flip turkey first on the side then breast up. Brush breast with softened butter. Insert meat thermometer into the thickest part of the thigh during this final one-third of roasting time.
4. Crease a large piece of foil lengthwise to make a tent, and arrange it loosely over bird. Return to oven and continue roasting. The tent keeps turkey moist and prevents overbrowning. The turkey is done when thermometer registers 180° to 185°F, or the thickest part of drumstick feels soft when pressed with fingers protected with clean cloth or paper napkin.
5. Transfer turkey to a heated serving platter, lifting it with the foil band; remove band. Let turkey stand covered with the foil tent for about 30 minutes for easier carving; remove tent. Garnish platter with chutney filled oranges, or as desired.

*To make the band, fold a long piece of heavy-duty aluminum foil lengthwise over and over to make a 3 inch wide band.

# Stuffed Turkey

1   **turkey (12 to 16 pounds)**
    **Salt and pepper**
    **Juice of 1 lemon**
    **Stuffing**
    **Melted butter**

Gravy:
    **Flour**
    **Chicken broth**
    **White wine**
    **Salt and pepper**

1. Clean turkey. Sprinkle inside and out with salt and pepper, then drizzle with lemon juice.
2. Spoon desired amount of stuffing into cavities of turkey. Secure openings with skewers and twine.
3. Put turkey, breast side up, on a rack in a shallow roasting pan. Cover bird with a double thickness of cheesecloth soaked in butter.
4. Roast in a 325°F oven 4½ to 5½ hours, or until done (180°F to 185°F on a meat thermometer inserted in inside thigh muscle or thickest part of breast); baste with drippings several times during roasting.
5. For gravy, stir a small amount of flour with pan drippings. Cook until bubbly. Stir in equal parts of broth and wine. Season to taste with salt and pepper.
6. Put turkey on a platter and garnish with watercress. Accompany with gravy.

*12 to 16 servings*

# Roast Stuffed Turkey

| | |
|---|---|
| 1 | turkey (6 to 8 pounds) |
| 1 | package (7 ounces) herb-seasoned stuffing croutons |
| ½ | cup melted butter |
| ½ | cup hot water or chicken broth |
| 2 | tablespoons butter |
| ½ | cup chopped celery |
| ½ | cup chopped onion |
| 2 | tablespoons chopped parsley |
| | Melted butter |

1. Rinse turkey with cold water; pat dry.
2. Turn stuffing croutons into a bowl; add ½ cup melted butter and toss gently. Stir in hot water or broth.
3. Heat 2 tablespoons butter in a skillet. Add celery and onion; cook until tender. Add to bowl with stuffing; add parsley and toss to mix.
4. Spoon stuffing into cavities of bird. Place turkey, breast side up, in a large electric cooker. Insert a meat thermometer in inner thigh muscle. Brush with melted butter.
5. Cover and roast at 300°F until meat thermometer registers 180°-185°, about 6 hours.

*6 to 10 servings*

*Note:* If desired to enhance browning, place a piece of aluminum foil over turkey before covering with lid.

# Roast Goose

| | |
|---|---|
| 1 | ready-to-cook goose, 8 to 10 lbs. |
| 1 | tablespoon salt |
| ¼ | teaspoon black pepper |
| 1 | lb. cooking apples, pared and quartered |
| ¾ | lb. prunes (soaked in warm water, drained, and pitted) |
| 1 | tablespoon sugar |

1. Rinse goose and remove any large layers of fat from the body cavity. Pat dry with absorbent paper. Rub body and neck cavities with a mixture of the salt and pepper.
2. Mix apples, prunes, and sugar together; lightly spoon mixture into cavities. To close body cavity, sew, or skewer and lace with a cord. Fasten neck skin to back with skewer. Loop cord around legs, tighten slightly, and tie around a skewer inserted on the back above tail. Rub skin of goose with a little salt.
3. Place goose, breast down, on a rack in a shallow roasting pan.
4. Roast, uncovered, at 325°F 2½ hours, removing fat from pan several times during this period. Turn goose, breast up, and roast 45 to 60 minutes longer, or until goose tests done. To test for doneness, move leg gently by grasping end of bone. When done, drumstick-thigh joint moves easily or twists out.
5. Transfer goose to a carving board or heated serving platter while preparing Gravy, below. Garnish as desired.

*About 8 servings*

*Gravy:* Pour off all but ¼ cup of drippings from roasting pan. Add about 2 cups hot water; bring to boiling, stirring to loosen browned residue. Stir in a smooth mixture of ½ cup cold water and ¼ cup flour. Bring to boiling and boil 1 to 2 minutes, stirring constantly. Season to taste. If desired, add 2 tablespoons currant jelly and cooked giblets.

# Roast Goose With Prune Apple Stuffing

2   cups pitted cooked prunes
1   goose, 10 to 12 lbs. ready-to-cook weight
    Salt
6   medium (about 2 lbs.) apples

1. Set out a shallow roasting pan with rack.
2. Have ready pitted cooked prunes.
3. Reserve about 8 to 10 prunes for garnish.
4. Clean and remove any layers of fat from body cavity and opening of goose.
5. Cut of neck at body, leaving on neck skin. (If goose is frozen, thaw, following directions on package.) Rinse and pat dry with absorbent paper. (Reserve giblets for use in gravy or other food preparation.) Rub body and neck cavities of goose with salt.
6. Wash, quarter, core and pare apples.
7. Lightly fill body and neck cavities with the apples and prunes. To close body cavity, sew or skewer and lace with cord. Fasten neck skin to back with skewer. Loop cord around legs and tighten slightly. Place breast-side down on rack in roasting pan.
8. Roast uncovered at 325°F 3 hrs. Remove fat from pan is it accumulates during this period. Turn goose breast side up. Roast 1 to 2 hrs. longer, or until goose tests done. To test for doneness, move leg gently by grasping end of bone; drumstick-thigh joint should move easily. (Protect fingers with paper napkin.) Allow about 25 min. per pound to estimate total roasting time.
9. To serve, remove skewers and cord. Place goose on heated platter. Remove some of the apples from goose and arrange on the platter. Garnish with the reserved prunes and **watercress.** For an attractive garnish, place cooked **prunes** on top of cooked **apple rings** if desired.

*8 servings*

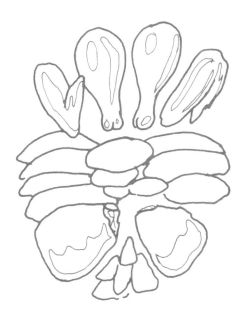

# Roast Capon

5   to 8lb. capon
    Salt
    Stuffing (your favorite recipe or a packaged stuffing mix)
    Melted fat

1. Prepare for stuffing (see Stuffing).
2. Rub body and neck cavities with salt.
3. Fill cavities lightly with Stuffing.
4. Fasten neck skin to back with a skewer and bring wing tips onto back. Push drumsticks under band or skin at tail, or tie with cord. Place breastside up on rack in shallow roasting pan. Brush with melted fat.
5. Roast at 325°F 2½ to 3½ hrs., or until thickest part of drumstick feels soft when pressed with fingers, basting frequently with melted fat or pan drippings.
6. When capon is two-thirds done, cut band of skin or cord at drumsticks. Roast until done. After removal from oven, allow capon to stand about 20 min., to make carving easier.
7. Prepare Gravy from the drippings, if desired.

*1 Stuffed capon*

# Roast Duckling A L'Orange

2   ready-to-cook ducklings,
     4 lbs. each
2   teaspoons salt
     Apricot-Rice Stuffing,
     page 45
1   cup orange juice
2   tablespoons butter or
     margarine
     Orange Gravy, below

1. Rinse ducklings and pat dry with absorbent paper. Rub cavities of ducklings with salt.
2. Prepare Apricot-Rice Stuffing and set aside.
3. Heat orange juice and butter together over low heat until butter is melted. Remove from heat and, using a pastry brush, brush cavities with the mixture.
4. Lightly fill body and neck cavities with the stuffing; do not pack. To close body cavities, sew, or skewer and lace with cord; fasten neck skin to backs and wings to bodies with skewers. Place ducklings, breast up, on rack in roasting pan. Brush with juice mixture.
5. Roast, uncovered, at 325°F 2½ to 3 hours. To test doneness, move leg gently by grasping end bone; drumstick-thigh joint should move easily. Brush frequently with orange juice mixture; pour off and reserve drippings as they accumulate.
6. Place ducklings on a heated platter; remove skewers and cord. Garnish with broiled orange slices and parsley; serve with Orange Gravy.

*6 to 8 servings*

*Orange Gravy:* Leaving brown residue in roasting pan, pour drippings and fat into a bowl. Allow fat to rise to surface; skim off fat and reserve 3 tablespoons; put reserved fat into roasting pan. Blend in 3 tablespoons flour, ¼ teaspoon salt, and ⅛ teaspoon black pepper. Stirring constantly, heat until mixture bubbles. Remove from heat. Continue to stir while slowly adding 2 cups reserved drippings plus orange juice. Return to heat and cook rapidly, stirring constantly, until gravy thickens. Cook 1 to 2 minutes longer. While stirring, scrape bottom and sides of pan to blend in brown residue. Blend in ⅓ cup orange marmalade. Remove from heat; pour into gravy boat and serve hot.

# Duckling, Southern Style

2   tablespoons butter
1   tablespoon flour
2   tablespoons chopped ham
¾   teaspoon salt
⅛   teaspoon pepper
     Paprika
2   tablespoons minced onion
½   cup chopped celery
2   tablespoons chopped
     green pepper
1   tablespoon chopped
     parsley
1½  cups bouillon or con-
     somme
1   whole clove
¼   teaspoon mace
2   cups diced cooked duck-
     ling

1. Melt butter in cooking pan of a chafing dish. Stir in flour and ham. Blend in salt, pepper, paprika, onion, celery, green pepper, and parsley.
2. Gradually stir in bouillon; add clove and mace. Simmer 15 minutes.
3. Stir in cooked duck and place over simmering water. Heat thoroughly and serve with fried hominy or mush.

*4 servings*

# Pasta & Rice

## Lasagne I

**Tomato Sauce with Meat (page 47)**
3  tablespoons olive oil
1  pound ground beef
1  pound lasagne noodles, cooked and drained
¾  pound mozzarella cheese, thinly sliced
2  hard-cooked eggs, sliced
¼  cup grated Parmesan cheese
½  teaspoon pepper
1  cup ricotta

1. Prepare sauce, allowing 4½ hours for cooking.
2. Heat olive oil in a skillet. Add ground beef and cook until browned, separating into small pieces.
3. Spread ½ cup sauce in a 2-quart baking dish. Top with a layer of noodles and half the mozzarella cheese. Spread half the ground beef and half the egg slices on top. Sprinkle on half the Parmesan cheese and ¼ teaspoon pepper. Top with ½ cup ricotta.
4. Beginning with sauce, repeat layering, ending with ricotta. Top ricotta with ½ cup sauce. Arrange over this the remaining lasagne noodles. Top with more sauce.
5. Bake at 350°F about 30 minutes, or until mixture is bubbling. Let stand 5 to 10 minutes to set the layers. Cut in squares and serve topped with remaining sauce.

*6 to 8 servings*

## Lasagne II

**Tomato Sauce with Meat (page 47)**
1  pound lasagne noodles, cooked, drained, and rinsed
2  pounds ricotta
1  pound mozzarella or scamorze cheese, shredded
1  cup shredded Parmesan cheese

1. Prepare Tomato Sauce with Meat.
2. Spread about 1 cup tomato sauce in a buttered 13x9x2-inch baking dish. Using a fourth of each, add a layer of noodles and then one of tomato sauce. Using a third of each, top evenly with 3 cheeses. Repeat layering and end with sauce.
3. Heat in a 375°F oven about 30 minutes, or until bubbly. Allow to stand 10 to 15 minutes to set layers before serving. Cut into squares.

*12 to 15 servings*

# Egg Noodles with Poppy Seed

| | |
|---|---|
| 1½ | quarts boiling water |
| 1 | teaspoon salt |
| 3 | cups egg noodles |
| ½ | cup milk |
| ½ | cup poppy seed, ground |
| 3 | tablespoons sugar or 2 tablespoons honey |

1. Combine boiling water and salt in a large saucepan. Add noodles and cook until tender. Drain.
2. Meanwhile, scald milk; mix in poppy seed and sugar. Cook 5 minutes.
3. Combine poppy seed mixture with the noodles. Serve hot.

*4 to 6 servings*

# Meat-Stuffed Manicotti

| | |
|---|---|
| 2 | tablespoons olive oil |
| ½ | pound fresh spinach, washed, dried, and finely chopped |
| 2 | tablespoons chopped onion |
| ½ | teaspoon salt |
| ½ | teaspoon oregano |
| ½ | pound ground beef |
| 2 | tablespoons fine dry bread crumbs |
| 1 | egg, slightly beaten |
| 1 | can (6 ounces) tomato paste |
| 8 | manicotti shells (two thirds of a 5½-ounce package), cooked and drained |
| 1½ | tablespoons butter, softened (optional) |
| 2 | tablespoons grated Parmesan or Romano cheese (optional) Mozzarella cheese, shredded |

1. Heat olive oil in a skillet. Add spinach, onion, salt, oregano, and meat. Mix well, separating meat into small pieces. Cook, stirring frequently, until meat is no longer pink.
2. Set aside to cool slightly. Add bread crumbs, egg, and 2 tablespoons tomato paste; mix well. Stuff manicotti with mixture. Put side by side in a greased 2-quart baking dish. If desired, spread butter over stuffed manicotti and sprinkle with the grated cheese.
3. Spoon remaining tomato paste on top of the manicotti down the center of the dish. Sprinkle mozzarella cheese on top of tomato paste. Cover baking dish.
4. Bake at 425°F 12 to 15 minutes, or until mozzarella melts.

*4 servings*

# Peas in Rice Ring

| | |
|---|---|
| 1 | package (6 or 6¾ ounces) seasoned wild and white rice mix |
| 3 | pounds fresh peas Butter |

1. Cook rice mix according to package directions.
2. Meanwhile, rinse and shell peas just before cooking to retain their delicate flavor. Cook covered in boiling salted water to cover for 15 to 20 minutes, or until peas are tender. Drain and add just enough butter so peas glisten.
3. Butter a 1-quart ring mold. When rice is done, turn into mold, packing down gently with spoon. Invert onto a warm serving platter and lift off mold.
4. Spoon hot peas into rice ring just before serving.

*About 6 servings*

# Stuffing

## Turkey Stuffing

4 slices toasted bread, crumbled
1 medium-sized pan corn-bread, crumbled
Turkey stock
6 eggs
1 stalk celery, chopped
3 large onions, chopped
¼ cup butter

1. Mix toast and cornbread crumbs with enough turkey stock so that mixture will not be stiff.
2. Add the eggs, celery, onion, and butter. Season to taste with salt, pepper, and sage.
3. Bake at 325°F about 1 hour.

*8 servings*

## Wine Stuffing For Turkey

3 qts. bread cubes
2 cups chopped blanched almonds
4 cups diced celery
2 cups chopped celery leaves
¼ cup butter or margarine
½ cup finely chopped green onion
2 cloves garlic, minced
3 eggs, slightly beaten
1 tablespoon salt
¼ teaspoon cracked black pepper
½ teaspoon ground nutmeg
½ teaspoon ground mace
½ cup dry red wine

1. Combine the bread cubes, almonds, celery, and celery leaves; toss lightly until well mixed.
2. Heat the butter in a skillet. Add the green onion and garlic and cook, stirring occasionally, until lightly browned. Add contents of skillet to bread mixture.
3. Combine the eggs, salt, pepper, nutmeg, and mace. Pour egg mixture and wine over bread cubes; toss lightly to mix thoroughly.
4. Lightly spoon into body and neck cavities of turkey (do not pack).

*About 16 cups stuffing*

# Old-Fashioned Cornbread Stuffing

1   cup dark or golden seedless raisins
1½  cups thinly sliced celery
8   cups soft white-bread crumbs
6   cups cornbread crumbs
1   cup coarsely chopped salted toasted almonds
½   cup chopped parsley
1   teaspoon poultry seasoning
1   teaspoon ground nutmeg
1   teaspoon salt
½   teaspoon pepper
⅔   cup giblet broth
½   cup instant minced onion
¾   cup butter or margarine, melted
2   eggs, beaten

1. Combine raisins, celery, crumbs, almonds, and parsley. Sprinkle with a mixture of the poultry seasoning, nutmeg, salt, and pepper.
2. Add broth and onion to butter; add butter mixture and eggs to crumb mixture, mixing lightly.
3. Spoon mixture lightly into turkey; or shape into stuffing balls, place on greased baking sheet, and bake at 350°F 20 minutes, or until lightly browned.

*Stuffing for a 15-pound Turkey or 20 Balls*

# Wild Rice Stuffing

1   cup wild rice, cooked
½   lb. fresh mushrooms, sliced
2   tablespoons chopped onion
½   cup butter or margarine
½   teaspoon crushed sage leaves (optional)
    Dash thyme (optional)

1. While wild rice is cooking, lightly brown the mushrooms with onion in ¼ cup heated butter in a skillet. Toss gently with the wild rice and herbs.
2. Add remaining ¼ cup butter, melted, and continue tossing until thoroughly mixed. Add salt and pepper to taste.

*About 4 cups stuffing*

# Potato And Celery Stuffing

2   onions
2   tablespoons melted butter
½   cup pork sausage
¼   cup chopped celery leaves
5   large uncooked potatoes
2   stalks celery
1   teaspoon salt
½   teaspoon paprika

1. Dice 1 onion and saute in butter until golden brown.
2. Add sausage and celery leaves and cook 2 minutes.
3. Pare potatoes and put through food chopper with celery stalks and remaining onion. Add to cooked mixture wsith salt and paprika and mix well. Will fill a 3 to 4-pound fowl.

*Country Potato Stuffing*—Use 3 cups hot mashed potatoes instead of uncooked potatoes. Use only 1 onion; omit butter. Dice celery and onion and mix all ingredients together without sauteing. Add ½ cup bread crumbs; 1 egg, beaten; ¼ cup cream and ½ teaspoon mustard. Mix together thoroughly and use to stuff poultry or crown roast of lamb or pork.

# Fruit Stuffing For Goose

| | |
|---|---|
| 3 | cups bread cubes |
| ½ | cup fat, melted |
| 1 | cup chopped apples |
| ½ | cup chopped cooked prunes |
| ½ | cup chopped nuts |
| 1 | teaspoon salt |
| ¼ | teaspoon pepper |
| 1 | tablespoon lemon juice |

Mix all ingredients lightly. Will fill a 4 to 5 pound goose.

# Apricot-Rice Stuffing

| | |
|---|---|
| ¼ | cup orange juice |
| ¼ | cup butter or margarine, melted |
| ½ | teaspoon salt |
| ¼ | teaspoon pepper |
| ⅛ | teaspoon thyme |
| ⅛ | teaspoon ground nutmeg |
| ⅛ | teaspoon ground cloves |
| 3½ | cups cooked rice |
| 1 | cup finely chopped dried apricots |
| ¼ | cup finely chopped onion |
| ¼ | cup finely chopped celery |
| 2 | tablespoons finely chopped parsley |

Combine all ingredients in a large bowl. Toss lightly until thoroughly mixed.

*About 5 cups stuffing*

# Walnut Stuffing

| | |
|---|---|
| 2 | pkgs. (7 to 8 oz. each) herb-seasoned stuffing mix |
| ¾ | cup butter or margarine, melted |
| 2 | cups chicken broth |
| 1 | can (6 oz.) broiled sliced mushrooms, undrained |
| 1½ | cups chopped toasted walnuts |

Toss stuffing mix with the melted butter in a bowl. Lightly mix in remaining ingredients.

*Stuffing for a 14 to 16-pound turkey*

# Dressings & Sauces

## Medium White Sauce

| | |
|---|---|
| 2 | **tablespoons butter** |
| 2 | **tablespoons flour** |
| 1 | **cup milk** |
| ¼ | **teaspoon salt** |
| ⅛ | **teaspoon pepper** |

*Method 1*—Melt butter and blend in flour. Add milk gradually, stirring constantly. Reduce heat and cook 3 minutes longer; add seasonings.

*Method 2*—Blend butter and flour together and add to hot milk, stirring constantly until mixture thickens. Cook 3 minutes longer; add seasonings.

*Cream Sauce:* Use cream for milk.

*Thin White Sauce:* Use 1 tablespoon butter and 1 tablespoon flour.

## Whipped Cream Dressing

| | |
|---|---|
| ⅔ | **cup sugar** |
| 2 | **tablespoons flour** |
| 2 | **eggs, beaten** |
| 2 | **tablespoons salad oil** |
| 3 | **tablespoons lemon juice** |
| 4 | **tablespoons orange juice** |
| 1 | **cup pineapple juice** |
| ½ | **cup heavy cream, whipped** |

1. Combine sugar and flour in top of double boiler.
2. Add remaining ingredients except cream and cook until thickened, stirring constantly.
3. When cool, fold in whipped cream.

*Makes 2 cups*

# French Dresing

| | |
|---|---|
| 1 | cup olive or salad oil |
| ¼ | cup vinegar |
| ½ | teaspoon salt |
| | Few grains cayenne |
| ¼ | teaspoon white pepper |
| 2 | tablespoons chopped parsley |

1. Combine all ingredients.
2. Beat or shake thoroughly before using.

*Makes 1¼ cups*

# Lime French Dressing

| | |
|---|---|
| ½ | cup olive or salad oil |
| ¼ | cup lime juice |
| ¼ | cup lemon juice |
| ½ | teaspoon salt |
| | Few grains cayenne |
| 2 | tablespoons sugar or honey |

1. Combine all ingredients.
2. Shake well before using.

*Makes 1 cup*

# Tomato Sauce with Meat

| | |
|---|---|
| ¼ | cup plus 3 tablespoons olive oil |
| ½ | cup (about 1 medium) chopped onion |
| ½ | lb. beef chuck |
| ½ | lb. pork shoulder |
| ½ | lb. ground beef |
| 7 | cups canned tomatoes, sieved |
| 1 | tablespoon salt |
| 1 | bay leaf |
| ¾ | cup (6-oz. can) tomato paste |

1. Set out a large saucepot with a tight-fitting cover.
2. Heat ¼ cup olive oil in sauceppot.
3. Add chopped onion and cook until lightly browned.
4. Add beef chuck and pork shoulder to skillet and cook, turning occasionally, until browned.
5. Add slowly a mixture of tomatoes, salt and bay leaf. Cover saucepot and simmer over very low heat, about 2½ hrs.
6. Simmer uncovered over very low heat, stirring occasionally, about 2 hrs., or until thickened. If sauce becomes too thick, add ½ cup water.
7. Meanwhile, brown ground beef in 3 tablespoons olive oil, separating beef into small pieces with fork or spoon.
8. Remove beef chuck, pork shoulder and bay leaf from sauce.
9. Add ground beef to sauce and simmer 10 min. longer. Serve over cooked spaghetti.

*About 4 cups sauce*

*Tomato Sauce with Mushrooms:* Follow recipe for Tomato Sauce with Ground Meat. Clean and slice **½ lb. mushrooms.** Cook slowly in **3 tablespoons melted butter** until lightly browned. After removing meat from sauce, add mushrooms and cook 10 min longer.

# Tomato Sauce

| | |
|---|---|
| 1 | clove garlic |
| 2 | tablespoons olive oil |
| 3 | pounds fully ripe plum tomatoes, peeled, seeded, and diced; or use 9 cups, canned peeled plum tomatoes, sieved |
| 1 | teaspoon salt |
| ¼ | teaspoon freshly ground black pepper |
| 1 | tablespoon dried basil |

1. Peel garlic and cut in thirds. Put into a deep skillet with olive oil. Heat until garlic is browned. Flatten garlic and move it around in the oil. Discard garlic.
2. Add tomatoes all at one time to skillet. Mix in salt, pepper, and basil. Cook over low heat, stirring occasionally, about 10 minutes. Continue cooking, stirring occasionally, until sauce thickens (about 20 minutes).

*About 6 cups sauce*

# Clam Sauce

| | |
|---|---|
| ¼ | cup finely chopped onion |
| 3 | tablespoons butter |
| 2 | tablespoons flour |
| ¼ | teaspoon salt |
| ⅛ | teaspoon white pepper |
| 1 | can (12 ounces) clam juice |
| 3 | tablespoons finely chopped parsley |
| ½ | teaspoon thyme |
| 1 | jar (7½ ounces) whole clams, drained and cut in pieces |
| 1 | can (2½ ounces) minced clams, drained |

1. Add onion to hot butter in a saucepan and cook until soft. Blend in a mixture of flour, salt and pepper. Heat until bubbly.
2. Remove from heat and add the clam juice gradually, stirring constantly. Mix in parsley and thyme. Bring to boiling; stir and cook 1 to 2 minutes. Stir in the clams; heat thoroughly.

*About 2¼ cups sauce*

# Bearnaise Sauce

| | |
|---|---|
| 4 | egg yolks |
| 1 | cup butter |
| 1 | tablespoon lemon juice |
| 1 | tablespoon tarragon vinegar |
| ¼ | teaspoon salt |
| 1 | teaspoon chopped parsley |
| 1 | teaspoon onion juice |
| | Dash cayenne |

1. Place egg yolks with ⅓ of butter in top of double boiler.
2. Keep water in bottom of boiler hot but not boiling.
3. Add remaining butter as sauce thickens, stirring constantly.
4. Remove from heat and add remaining ingredients.
5. Serve with broiled meat.

*Makes 1 cup*

# Cakes & Pies

# Old Williamsburg-Style Fruitcake

1 cup butter or margarine
2⅓ cups sugar
4 egg yolks
4 cups sifted all-purpose flour
½ cup sherry
1 lb. walnuts, chopped
1 pkg. (15 oz.) golden raisins
8 oz. (1 cup) finely chopped candied red cherries
8 oz. (1⅓ cups) diced candied pineapple
8 oz. (1 cup) diced candied citron
2 cups flaked coconut, finely chopped
4 egg whites, beaten to stiff, not dry, peaks
Almond Paste, below
Icing, below

1. Cream butter. Gradually add sugar, beating thoroughly after each addition. Add egg yolks, one at a time, beating until light and fluffy after each addition. Blend in 1 cup flour, then the sherry.
2. Mix the remaining flour, walnuts, the fruits, and coconut. Stir into mixture in bowl. Fold in beaten egg whites. Turn batter into a greased 10-inch tubed pan lined with greased brown paper or baking parchment. Spread evenly in pan.
3. Bake at 300°F 2¾ hours, or until cake tests done.
4. Cool completely on wire rack before removing the cake from the pan.
5. Brush cake with *sherry*. Wrap tightly in aluminum foil. Store in a cool place.
6. The day before the cake is to be served, brush top and sides of cake with a slightly beaten *egg white*. Place the round of Almond Paste on top of the cake and arrange pieces on sides; press edges to seal. Let dry at room temperature about 8 hours.
7. Reserving about 1 cup, spread Icing over sides and top of cake. Using a pastry bag and tube, decorate with reserved icing. Garnish with *flaked coconut* and *candied red and green cherries*. Let dry at room temperature about 4 hours.

One 10-Pound Decorated Fruitcake

*Almond Paste:* Blend *1 pound (about 4 cups) ground blanched almonds, 1 pound confectioners' sugar, 3 egg whites, 1 tablespoon lemon juice, ½ teaspoon orange extract, and ⅛ teaspoon almond extract.* Press into a ball. Roll out about one third of the ball into an 8-inch round on waxed paper dusted with *confectioners' sugar*. Roll remainder of ball into a 28x4-inch strip; cut into 4 pieces.

*Icing:* Add *3 cups confectioners' sugar* to *2 egg whites* and beat with electric mixer at high speed about 5 minutes. Blend in *2 tablespoons lemon juice*. Add *3 cups confectioners' sugar* gradually, beating the mixture well.

# Holiday Fruitcake

1½    **cups sifted all-purpose flour**
1    **teaspoon baking powder**
1    **teaspoon cinnamon**
½    **teaspoon ginger**
½    **teaspoon nutmeg**
⅛    **teasppoon salt**
1    **cup chopped mixed candied fruit (6 ounces)**
1    **cup raisins (5 ounces)**
¾    **cup chopped walnuts**
½    **cup butter or margarine**
¾    **cup packed brown sugar**
1    **egg**
½    **cup beer**
   **Halved candied cherries (optional)**

1. Sift together dry ingredients. Mix a little with fruits and nuts.
2. Cream butter and brown sugar. Add egg; beat well.
3. Add remaining dry ingredients alternately with beer; beat until smooth.
4. Add fruits and nuts; stir by hand.
5. Turn into greased and waxed-paper-lined pans: three 5½x3x2-inch fruitcake pans, or one 9x5x3-inch loaf pan. Decorate tops with candied cherries, if desired.
6. Bake at 275°F 1¼ hours for small pans, or 1¾ to 2 hours for a 9x5-inch pan, or until done. Cool 20 minutes in pans. Turn out on wire racks.
7. Wrap each fruitcake in cheesecloth soaked in additional beer, then wrap in foil. Age in refrigerator at least 2 weeks, basting occasionally with beer.

*3 small or 1 large*

# Dark Fruitcake

2    **pounds seeded raisins, chopped**
1¾    **pounds sultana raisins, chopped**
¾    **pound citron, chopped**
1    **pound currants**
½    **pound candied pineapple**
¼    **cup chopped candied lemon peel**
½    **pound candied cherries, halved**
¼    **cup chopped candied orange peel**
1    **cup grape juice**
2    **cups chopped nut meats**
1    **pound cake flour**
2    **cups shortening**
1    **pound brown sugar**
12    **eggs**
1    **cup molasses**
4    **teaspoons cinnamon**
4    **teaspoons allspice**
1½    **teaspoons mace**
½    **teaspoon nutmeg**
½    **teaspoon baking soda**
½    **teaspoon salt**
4    **ounces (squares) chocolate, melted**
2    **tablespoons hot water**

1. Combine fruit. Pour grape juice over fruit and let stand overnight.
2. Dredge fruit and nuts with half of the flour.
3. Cream shortening and sugar until fluffy.
4. Add eggs, 1 at a time, to the creamed mixture and continue creaming. Add molasses.
5. Combine remaining flour with other dry ingredients and sift 3 times. Add alternately with grape juice and fruit mixture to creamed sugar and egg mixture.
6. Add chocolate and hot water. Blend thoroughly.
7. Pour into greased loaf pans lined with brown paper.
8. Steam for 2 hours and bake in slow oven 300°F for an additional 1½ hours.
9. Cakes may be decorated with pieces of fruit before placing in oven.
10. Peel paper from cakes while warm.

*8 10x2x3-inch loaves*

# Pecan Fruitcake

1   lb. (about 2½ cups) candied red cherries, cut in pieces
1   lb. (about 3 cups) golden raisins
1   lb. (about 4 cups) pecans, coarsely chopped
4   cups sifted all-purpose flour
2   teaspoons baking powder
2   cups butter or margarine
4   teaspoons lemon juice
2¼   cups sugar
6   large eggs

1. Combine cherries, raisins, pecans, and 1 cup of the flour. Blend the remaining flour and baking powder; set aside.
2. Cream butter with lemon juice. Add sugar gradually, creaming until fluffy after each addition. Add eggs, one at a time, beating thoroughly after each addition.
3. Beating only until smooth after each addition, add dry ingredients in fourths to creamed mixture. Blend in the fruit mixture. Turn batter into a well greased 10-inch tubed pan and spread evenly.
4. Place a shallow pan containing water on bottom rack of oven during baking time.
5. Bake at 275°F about 4½ hours, or until cake tests done.
6. Remove from oven to wire rack. Remove from pan before entirely cooled. Cool completely.

About 7 Pounds Fruitcake

# Unbaked Fruitcake

8   oz. (1½ cups) raisins
1   cup chopped figs
1   cup chopped dried pears
1   cup chopped walnuts
6   oz. (1 cup) chopped candied pineapple
6   oz. (1 cup) chopped candied cherries
4   oz. (½ cup) chopped candied citron
8   oz. (1 cup) chopped candied orange peel
¾   cup butter or margarine
1   tablespoon grated orange peel
¾   cup confectioners' sugar
3   doz. vanilla wafers finely crushed (about 7 cups crumbs)
¼   teaspoon salt
1   cup honey

1. Pour 2 cups boiling water over dried fruits; bring to boiling and drain. Mix with walnuts and candied fruits.
2. Cream butter with orange peel; gradually add confectioners' sugar, creaming well. Blend in crumbs, salt and honey. Mix with fruit-nut mixture. Press into a well-greased 2-quart fluted mold.
3. Refrigerate 2 to 3 days before unmolding to serve.

About 5 Pounds Fruitcake

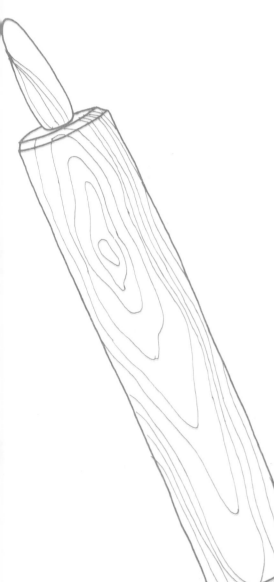

## Helpful Hints About Cakes

• Use fluted paper baking cups when preparing cupcakes. They save greasing of pans and eliminate sticking. They also make pan washing easy.

• Line cake pans with baking parchment or waxed paper for easy removal of cakes after baking. Grease pans (bottoms only) before lining with paper and grease the paper. Cut several pieces at one time to fit pans and keep on hand for future use. (Cut the circles for layer cake pans about ¼ inch smaller than size of pan.) After baked cakes are removed from pans, peel off paper immediately.

• For baking fruitcake, line the pan with heavy brown paper extending 1 inch above top of pan. When cake is baked, place on wire rack. When completely cooled, lift cake from pan and peel off paper.

• When baking an upside-down cake, line cake pan with aluminum foil, folding foil over the edges of pan. After cake is baked, let cool on rack about 5 minutes. Then place serving plate on top of cake, turn cake upside down and remove the pan. Carefully lift off the foil. Cake comes out of pan easily and pan is easy to clean.

• When making cakes (or cookies) which use shortening and call for flavoring extracts and/or ground spices, add them to the shortening before creaming with the sugar. The fat "carries" the extract and spice flavors through the batter.

• To make a lace-like decoration on a sponge or angel food cake or other unfrosted cake, place a sheer, lace paper doily on top of cake; sift confectioners' sugar over top; then carefully lift off doily.

• To make your own cinnamon sugar to be used for sprinkling over warm, not-to-be-frosted cakes and cupcakes, combine ½ *cup fine granulated sugar with 1 tablespoon ground cinnamon.* Keep the mixture on hand stored in a covered jar.

• If cooked white frosting has "sugared" somewhat, beat in a small amount of *lemon juice* until frosting is smooth.

• To make marshmallow flowers for cake decorating, use large white or colored *marshmallows.* With kitchen shears dipped in water, cut off strips about 1/8 inch thick. Place strips between 2 pieces of waxed paper and roll with rolling pin to make thin "petals." Arrange petals on frosted cake to simulate flowers.

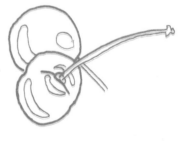

# Light Fruitcake

| | |
|---|---|
| 5 | cups white raisins |
| 2 | cups chopped dried white figs |
| 5 | cups sliced citron |
| 2 | cups halved candied cherries |
| ½ | cup fruit juice |
| 2 | teaspoons cardamom seeds |
| 3 | teaspoons nutmeg |
| 4 | teaspoons mace |
| 1 | teaspoon cinnamon |
| 1½ | cups thick Orange Marmalade |
| 4½ | cups sifted flour |
| 3 | teaspoons baking powder |
| 1½ | teaspoons salt |
| 2 | cups shortening |
| 2½ | cups sugar |
| 8 | eggs |
| 1 | teaspoon vanilla |
| 2 | teaspoons lemon extract |
| 1½ | cups chopped Brazil nuts |
| 2 | cups broken walnut meats |

1. Rinse fruits, drain and dry on towel. (If figs are very dry, let stand in hot water about 5 minutes.) Cut figs into thin strips.
2. Combine fruit juice and spices; mix and pour over combined fruit.
3. Add marmalade and mix well. Cover and let stand overnight.
4. Sift flour, baking powder and salt together.
5. Cream shortening and sugar until fluffy.
6. Add beaten eggs and mix.
7. Add flour, fruit mixture, flavoring and nuts and stir until fruit is well distributed.
8. Pour into 2 9-inch tube-cake pans which have been lined with 2 thicknesses of greased brown paper.
9. Smooth tops and decorate if desired.
10. Bake in very slow oven 275°F 3¾ to 4 hours.
11. Test with toothpick or cake tester before removing from oven.
12. May be used as soon as cool or ripened. Baked weight is approximately 9¾ pounds.

*Bite-Size Fruitcakes:* Follow and prepare one-half recipe from Light Fruitcake. Brush about 6 doz. 1¼-in. paper souffle cups with **salad oil** or **melted shortening.** Fill with about 1 tablespoon of batter. Decorate with bits of **red or green candied cherries.** Arrange, with space between cups, on baking sheet on which double thickness of wet paper toweling has been placed. Bake at 300°F about 30 min., or until cakes test done. Glaze before serving.

# Cherry Fruitcake

| | |
|---|---|
| 1½ | cups sifted all-purpose flour |
| 1½ | cups sugar |
| 1 | teaspoon baking powder |
| 1 | teaspoon salt |
| 2 | pkgs. (7¼ oz. each) pitted dates |
| 1 | lb. diced candied pineapple |
| 2 | jars (16 oz. each) red maraschino cherries, drained |
| 18 | oz. (about 5½ cups) pecan halves |
| 6 | eggs |
| ½ | cup dark rum |
| ½ | cup light corn syrup |

1. Grease two 9x5x3-in. loaf pans; line with aluminum foil, allowing a 2-in. overhang; grease the foil.
2. Sift flour, sugar, baking powder and salt, into a large mixing bowl.
3. Add pitted dates, pineapple, maraschino cherries and pecan halves to flour mixture and toss until coated.
4. Beat eggs in a bowl until thick.
5. Blend in rum.
6. Pour over fruit mixture and toss until thoroughly mixed. Turn into prepared loaf pans, pressing mixture with spatula to pack tightly.
7. Bake at 300°F about 1¾ hrs., or until wooden pick inserted in center of loaves comes out clean.
8. Remove from oven to cooling rack and allow to cool 15 min. before removing loaves from pans. Peel off foil and while still warm brush loaves with corn syrup.
9. Cool thoroughly before serving or storing.

*2 loaves fruitcake*

# Filled Holiday Coffee Cake

| | |
|---|---|
| **2** | **pkgs. active dry yeast** |
| **1** | **cup milk, scalded and cooled to warm** |
| **4** | **cups all-purpose flour** |
| **½** | **cup sugar** |
| **1** | **teaspoon salt** |
| **1** | **cup firm butter** |
| **2** | **eggs, beaten** |
| **1** | **teaspoon vanilla extract Vanilla-Butter Filling, above** |
| **1** | **cup chopped nuts Confectioners' Sugar Icing** |

1. Soften yeast in the cooled milk.

2. Mix flour, sugar, and salt in a large bowl. Cut in the butter with a pastry blender until particles are the size of rice kernels. Mixing well after each addition, add the yeast, then the mixture of eggs and extract.

3. Cover bowl with moisture-vaporproof material. Chill several hours or overnight.

4. Before removing dough from refrigerator, prepare Vanilla-Butter Filling. Spread 2 tablespoons filling over bottom and sides of each of two 9x5x3-inch loaf pans.

5. Divide dough into halves. On a lightly floured surface, roll each portion into an 18x10-inch rectangle. Spread each with half of remaining filling and sprinkle with half of nuts. Cut rectangle into three 10x6-inch strips. Starting with long side, roll up each strip and twist slightly. Braid three rolls together and place one braid in each pan, being sure to tuck ends under. Brush tops with *melted butter*.

6. Cover; let rise in a warm place until doubled, about 1½ hours.

7. Bake at 350°F 45 to 50 minutes. Immediately remove from pans and cool on wire racks.

8. Spread coffee cakes with Confectioners' Sugar Icing II. Before icing is set, decorate top with *marzipan fruit, glazed dried apricots,* and *preserved kumquats.*

*2 Filled Coffee Cakes*

*Confectioners' Sugar Icing:* Blend 1 cup confectioners' sugar, 1 tablespoon softened butter, 1 teaspoon light corn syrup, and 1 tablespoon hot water.

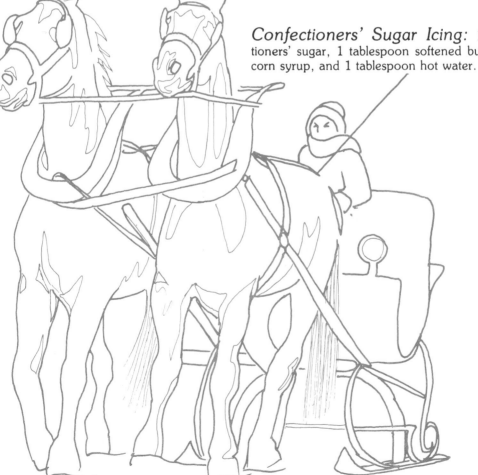

# Black Forest Torte

| | |
|---|---|
| 1½ | cups toasted filberts, grated* |
| ¼ | cup flour |
| ½ | cup butter or margarine |
| 1 | cup sugar |
| 6 | egg yolks |
| 4 | oz. (4 sq.) semisweet chocolate, melted and cooled |
| 6 | tablespoons kirsch |
| 6 | eggs whites |
| | Cherry Filling, below |
| 3 | cups chilled heavy cream |
| ⅓ | cup confectioners' sugar |
| | Chocolate curls |

1. Grease and lightly flour an 8-inch springform pan; set aside.
2. Blend grated filberts and flour; set aside.
3. Cream butter until softened. Beat in sugar gradually until mixture is light and fluffy. Add egg yolks, one at a time, beating thoroughly after each addition.
4. Blend in the chocolate and 2 tablespoons of the kirsch. Stir in nut-flour mixture until blended.
5. Beat egg whites until stiff, not dry, peaks are formed. Formed. Fold into batter and turn into the pan.
6. Bake at 375°F about 1 hour, or until torte tests done. (Torte should be about 1½ inches high and top may have slight crack.)
7. Cool 10 minutes in pan on a wire rack; remove from pan and cool.
8. Using a long sharp knife, carefully cut torte into 3 layers. Place top layer inverted on a cake plate; spread with Cherry Filling.
9. Whip cream (1½ cups at a time) until soft peaks are formed, gradually adding half of the confectioners' sugar and 2 tablespoons of the kirsch to each portion.
10. Generously spread some of the whipped cream over the Cherry Filling. Cover with second layer and remaining Cherry Filling. Spread generously with more whipped cream and top with third torte layer. Frost entire torte with remaining whipped cream.
11. Decorate torte with reserved cherries and chocolate curls.

*One 8-inch Torte*

*To grate nuts, use a rotary-type grater with hand-operated crank.

*Cherry Filling:* Drain 1 jar (16 ounces) red maraschino cherries, reserving ½ cup syrup. Set aside 13 cherries for decoration; slice remaining cherries. Set aside. Combine reserved syrup and 4 tablespoons kirsch. In a saucepan, gradually blend syrup mixture into 1½ tablespoons cornstarch. Mix in 1 tablespoon lemon juice. Stir over medium heat until mixture boils ½ minute. Mix in sliced cherries and cool.

*1⅓ Cups Filling*

# Holiday Delight

| | |
|---|---|
| ½ | cup butter |
| ¾ | cup sugar |
| 2 | eggs, unbeaten |
| 2 | cups, sifted cake flour |
| ¼ | teaspoon salt |
| 4 | teaspoons baking powder |
| 1½ | cups raspberry jam |
| ½ | cup blanched almonds, chopped |
| ½ | pint heavy cream, whipped |

1. Cream butter and sugar together until fluffy. Add eggs.
2. Sift flour, salt and baking powder together and add to first mixture.
3. Form into balls.
4. Place in buttered muffin pans and press around edges of pans. Fill center with mixture of jam and nuts and bake in hot oven (450°F) about 10 minutes.
5. Cool and serve with whipped cream.

*Serves 8*

# Hot Water Pastry

2 cups sifted flour
½ teaspoon baking powder
1 teaspoon salt
⅓ cup boiling water
⅔ cup shortening

1. Sift flour, baking powder and salt together.
2. Pour water over shortening and mix with fork until creamy, add flour mixture and mix into a dough.
3. Chill thoroughly and proceed as for Plain Pastry.

*1 9-inch dough crust pie or 2 9-inch single crust pies*

*Christmas Tree:* Mark to suggest branches and decorate with green sugar.

*Santa Claus:* Mark to suggest features and decorate wit red sugar.

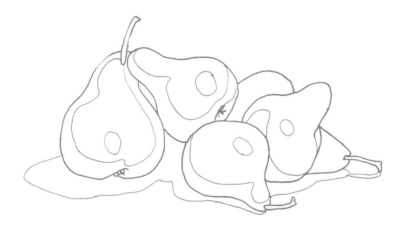

# Plain Pastry

2 cups sifted flour
¾ teaspoon salt
⅔ cup shortening
4 to 6 tablespoons cold water

1. Sift flour and salt together and cut in shortening with 2 knives or pastry blender.
2. Add water, using only a small portion at a time, until mixture will hold together.
3. Divide dough into 2 parts.
4. Roll out on floured board to desired size.
5. Line the piepan with one piece of dough, being careful not to stretch dough.
6. After filling is placed in pastry, dampen edges of lower crust with cold water and cover with remaining dough which has been rolled out and slashed in several places to allow steam to escape while baking.
7. Press edges together with prongs of fork and bake according to recipe for filling selected.

*2 9-inch shells for one 2-crust 9-inch pie*

*Christmas Tree:* Mark to suggest branches and decorate with green sugar.

*Santa Claus:* Mark to suggest features and decorate with red sugar.

# Mince Pie

| | |
|---|---|
| 1 | recipe Plain Pastry (page 56) |
| 2½ | cups mincemeat |

1. Line piepan with pastry, fill with mincemeat and cover with top crust.
2. Bake in hot oven 400°F about 35 minutes or until pastry is browned.
3. Serve hot.

*1 9-inch pie.*

# Mincemeat

| | |
|---|---|
| ¼ | lb. suet |
| 1½ | cups ground cooked lean beef |
| 4 | medium apples (about 3 cups, chopped) |
| 1 | cup firmly packed brown sugar |
| 1 | cup apple cider |
| ½ | cup fruit jelly |
| ½ | cup raisins, chopped |
| ½ | cup currants |
| 2 | tablespoons molasses |
| 1 | teaspoon salt |
| 1 | teaspoon cinnamon |
| ½ | teaspoon cloves |
| ½ | teaspoon nutmeg |
| ¼ | teaspoon mace |
| 1 | tablespoon grated lemon peel |
| 1 | tablespoon lemon juice |

1. Set out a large heavy skillet.
2. Put suet through medium blade of food chopper and add to ground meat. Set aside.
3. Wash, quarter, core, pare and chop apples.
4. Put apples and meat into skillet; add and mix brown sugar, apple cider, fruit jelly, raisins, currants and molasses.
5. Add mixture of salt, cinnamon, cloves, nutmeg and mace.
6. Stirring occasionally, simmer uncovered 1 hr., or until almost all of liquid is absorbed. Add lemon peel and lemon juice.
7. Blend thoroughly.

*3½ cups Mincemeat*

# Pumpkin Pie

| | |
|---|---|
| 1/8 | teaspoon salt |
| 2/3 | cup sugar |
| 2 | teaspoons pumpkin pie spice |
| 2 | eggs, slightly beaten |
| 1 2/3 | cups milk |
| 1½ | cups mashed cooked pumpkin |
| ½ | recipe Plain Pastry (page 56) |

1. Sift dry ingredients together and stir into eggs.
2. Add milk and pumpkin.
3. Line piepan with pastry and pour in filling.
4. Bake in very hot oven 450°F 10 minutes; reduce temperature to slow 325°F and bake 35 minutes longer or until knife inserted in center comes out clean. Cool.

*1 9-inch pie*

# Cookies

## Cinnamon Stars

| | |
|---|---|
| 6 | egg whites |
| 2 | teaspoons cinnamon |
| 2¾ | cups confectioners' sugar |
| 1 | pound almonds, not blanched |
| | Confectioners' sugar |

1. Mix egg whites, cinnamon and sugar until well blended. 2. Set aside ¼ cup for frosting.
3. Add finely ground almonds.
4. Roll out mixture on sugar-flour dusted board to ⅛ inch thick.
5. Cut with star cutter, frost with egg mixture stiffened with additional confectioners' sugar.
6. Bake at 300°F 20 minutes.

*60 cookies*

## Swiss Christmas Cookies

| | |
|---|---|
| 1¼ | cups strained honey |
| ¾ | cup shortening |
| 2 | cups sugar |
| ¼ | cup fruit juice |
| | Grated rind of 1 orange |
| | Grated rind of 1 lemon |
| 2 | cups unblanched almonds, chopped |
| 10 | cups cake flour |
| 1 | teaspoon salt |
| 1 | teaspoon cinnamon |
| 2 | teaspoons nutmeg |
| 1 | teaspoon cloves |
| 4 | teaspoons baking powder |

1. Melt honey and shortening together over hot water.
2. Add sugar and fruit juice and stir until dissolved.
3. Add grated rinds of orange and lemon, chopped almonds, and the dry ingredients which have been sifted together. Chill in refrigerator.
4. The dough may be kept several days to ripen or used at once. Roll about ⅛ of an inch thick and cut in strips about 2 by 2½ inches in size.
5. Bake in a slow oven 300°F 20 minutes. While still warm frost with Confectioners' Icing.

*180 cookies*

# Anise Form Cookies

2 eggs
1 cup sugar
½ teaspoon grated lemon peel
8 drops anise oil
2 cups sifted all-purpose flour
¼ teaspoon crushed ammonium carbonate (available at your pharmacy)

1. Beat eggs, sugar, lemon peel, and anise oil until very thick.
2. Blend flour and ammonium carbonate; add in fourths to egg-sugar mixture, mixing until blended after each addition.
3. Cover with a clean towel and let stand at room temperature 1 hour.
4. Shape dough into a ball and, on a floured surface, knead lightly with fingertips; roll ¼ inch thick.
5. Press lightly floured springerle rolling pin or mold firmly into dough to make clear designs.
6. Brush dough surface gently with soft brush to remove excess flour; cut the frames apart; cover and let stand 24 hours.
7. Lightly grease cookie sheets; sprinkle entire surface with **anise seed.**
8. Lightly brush back of each frame with water and set on anise seed.
9. Bake at 325°F 8 minutes.
10. When thoroughly cool, store in a tightly covered container 1 to 2 weeks before serving. To soften cookies, store for several days with a piece of apple or orange.

*About 4 dozen cookies*

# Holiday String-Ups

1 cup butter
2 teaspoons vanilla extract
1½ cups sugar
2 eggs
3¼ cups sifted all-purpose flour
1 teaspoon baking powder
½ teaspoon salt
Confectioners' Sugar Icing, (page 63)

1. Cream butter with extract; add sugar gradually, beating until fluffy. Add eggs, one at a time, beating thoroughly after each addition.
2. Sift flour, baking powder, and salt together; add to creamed mixture in fourths, mixing until blended after each addition. Chill dough thoroughly.
3. Roll a small amount of dough at a time ¼ inch thick on a floured surface; cut into a variety of shapes with cutters. Transfer to ungreased cookie sheets.
4. Insert 1-inch long pieces of paper straws or macaroni into top of each cutout, or press both ends of a piece of colored cord into the dough on the underside of each cutout.
5. Bake at 400°F 6 to 8 minutes.
6. Cool; gently twist out straws, leaving holes for ribbons or cord to be pulled through after decorating.
7. Prepare icing. Color with desired amount of **red** or **green food coloring.** Sprinkle with **decorative sugar.**

*About 5 dozen cookies*

*Note:* This versatile dough may be thinly rolled and baked cookies sandwiched together with filling.

*Chocolate String-Ups:* Follow recipe for Holiday String-Ups. Blend in **2 ounces (2 squares) unsweetened chocolate,** melted and cooled, after the eggs are added. Mix in **1 cup finely chopped pecans** after the last addition of dry ingredients.

# Mexican Christmas Cookies

| | |
|---|---|
| 1 | cup vegetable shortening |
| 2 | teaspoons grated orange peel |
| 1¼ | cups sugar |
| 1 | egg |
| ⅓ | cup fresh orange juice |
| 3¾ | cups all-purpose flour |
| ¼ | teaspoon salt |
| 1 | teaspoon cinnamon |
| ½ | teaspoon ground cloves |
| ½ | cup finely chopped pecans |
| | Very fine sugar |

1. Cream shortening, orange peel, and sugar until light. Beat in egg, then orange juice.
2. Blend flour, salt, and spices. Stir into creamed mixture. Mix in pecans.
3. Wrap dough and chill overnight.
4. Next day, roll out a small amount at a time on lightly floured surface to ⅛-inch thickness. Cut in desired shapes with fancy cookie cutter.
5. Put on lightly greased cookie sheets.
6. Bake at 375°F 8 to 10 minutes, or until golden brown.
7. Sprinkle with sugar while still warm.

*About 10 dozen*

# Almond Wreaths

| | |
|---|---|
| ¾ | cup butter |
| ½ | cup sugar |
| 1 | egg |
| 2 | cups sifted all-purpose flour |
| | Egg yolk, slightly beaten |
| ½ | cup blanched almonds, finely chopped |

1. Cream butter; add sugar gradually, beating until fluffy. Add egg and beat thoroughly.
2. Add flour in fourths, mixing until well blended after each addition. Chill dough thoroughly.
3. Roll one half of dough at a time ¼ inch-thick on a floured surface; cut with 1¾-inch round cutter and cut out centers with a ¾-inch round cutter. (Bake centers for samplers.)
4. Transfer rounds and rings to ungreased cookie sheets. Brush tops with egg yolk and sprinkle with almonds.
5. Bake at 350°F 10 to 15 minutes.

*About 6 dozen cookies*

# Basler Brunsli

| | |
|---|---|
| 1 | lb. unblanched almonds, grated* (5 cups) |
| 4 | to 4½ oz. (4 to 4½ sq.) unsweetened chocolate, grated* |
| 2½ | cups sugar |
| 1 | teaspoon ground cinnamon |
| 1 | tablespoon kirsch |
| 4 | egg whites (about ⅔ cup) |

1. Thoroughly blend almonds and chocolate with a mixture of sugar and cinnamon. Drizzle with the kirsch.
2. Beat the egg whites until stiff, not dry, peaks are formed. Blend into nut mixture. Chill thoroughly.
3. Roll a fourth of the mixture at a time ½ inch thick on a lightly sugared surface. Cut with 1¼-inch round cutter. Place on lightly greased cookie sheets.
4. Bake at 300°F 15 minutes. Cool on wire racks.

*About 10 dozen cookies*

*Blender grating speeds the job.

# Brandied Apricot Teacakes

8 ounces dried apricots, chopped
1 package (11 ounces) currants
½ cup boiling water
1 cup apricot brandy
½ cup butter
1½ cups firmly packed light brown sugar
3 eggs
2 cups all-purpose flour
½ teaspoon baking soda
½ teaspoon salt
1 teaspoon allspice
1 teaspoon cinnamon
1 teaspoon cloves
Confectioners' sugar

1. Put apricots and currants into a bowl; add water and brandy and mix well. Cover and let stand overnight.
2. Beat butter in a large bowl until softened. Add brown sugar gradually, creaming well. Add eggs, one at a time, and beat thoroughly after each addition.
3. Blend flour, baking soda, salt, and spices; add to creamed mixture gradually, mixing well. Blend in fruit mixture.
4. Set midget foil baking cups on baking sheets. Spoon a rounded tablespoonful of mixture into each cup.
5. Bake at 325°F about 30 minutes, or until a wooden pick inserted in cake comes out clean. Remove to wire rack to cool.
6. Before serving, sift confectioners' sugar over cakes.

*About 5 dozen teacakes*

*Note:* For smaller teacakes without baking cups, use well-buttered 1¾-inch muffin pan wells. Spoon 1 tablespoon mixture into each well. Bake at 325°F about 20 minutes.

*About 7 dozen teacakes.*

# Holiday Spritz

| 1 | cup butter |
|---|---|
| ½ | teaspoon almond extract |
| ½ | cup sugar |
| 1 | egg |
| 2 | cups all-purpose flour |

1. Cream butter with almond extract. Add sugar gradually, creaming well. Add egg and beat thoroughly. Add flour gradually, mixing until blended.
2. Chill dough until easy to handle. Chill cookie press.
3. Following manufacturer's directions, fill cookie press with dough and form cookies of varied shapes directly onto cool ungreased cookie sheets. Decorate with **colored sugar** or **multicolored nonpareil decors.**
4. Bake at 350°F 8 to 10 minutes. Remove to wire racks to cool.

*8 to 9 dozen cookies*

*Semisweet Chocolate Spritz:* Melt **2 squares (2 ounces) semisweet chocolate** and set aside to cool. Follow recipe for Holiday Spritz; blend chocolate into creamed mixture. Proceed as directed.

# Almond Spritz

| 1¼ | cups butter |
|---|---|
| ⅔ | cup sugar |
| 3 | egg yolks (¼ cup) |
| ¼ | cup grated almonds |
| 2½ | cups sifted all-purpose flour |

1. Cream butter; add sugar gradually, beating until fluffy. Add egg yolks, one at a time, beating thoroughly after each addition.
2. Stir in almonds. Add flour in fourths, mixing until blended after each addition.
3. Following manufacturer's directions, fill a cookie press with dough and form cookies of varied shapes directly onto ungreased cookie sheets.
4. Bake at 375°F 8 to 10 minutes.

*About 6 dozen cookies*

# Swedish Sand Tarts

| | |
|---|---|
| 1 | cup butter |
| ¼ | teaspoon almond extract |
| ¾ | cup sugar |
| 1 | egg |
| 2 | cups sifted all-purpose flour |
| ⅓ | cup blanched almonds, finely chopped |

1. Cream butter with extract; add sugar gradually, beating until fluffy. Add egg and beat thoroughly.
2. Add flour in fourths, mixing until blended after each addition. Stir in almonds. Chill dough thoroughly.
3. Remove a small portion of dough at a time from refrigerator and, depending upon size of mold, place 1 or 2 teaspoonfuls in each sandbakelse mold (usually available in the housewares section of department stores); press firmly to cover bottom and sides of mold evenly. Set lined molds on cookie sheets.
4. Bake at 375°F 6 to 8 minutes.
5. Immediately invert molds onto a smooth surface; cool slightly.
6. To remove sand tart, hold mold and tap lightly but sharply with back of spoon. Remove molds and cool cookies. Invert and sift Vanilla Confectioners' Sugar (below) over cookies.

*About 5 dozen cookies*

*Vanilla Confectioners' Sugar:* Cut a vanilla bean lengthwise, then crosswise, into pieces. Poke pieces into *1 to 2 pounds confectioners' sugar* at irregular intervals. Cover tightly and store. (The longer sugar stands, the richer the flavor.) When necessary, add more sugar. Replace vanilla bean when aroma is gone. Flavor *granulated sugar* this way, also.

# Lemon Sugar Cookies

| | |
|---|---|
| ¾ | cup butter |
| 1 | teaspoon grated lemon peel |
| 1 | tablespoon lemon juice |
| 1¼ | cups sugar |
| 2 | eggs |
| 2 | cups sifted all-purpose flour |
| 1½ | teaspoons baking powder |
| ½ | teaspoon salt |

1. Cream butter with lemon peel and juice; add the sugar gradually, creaming until fluffy. Add the eggs, one at a time, beating thoroughly after each addition.
2. Sift flour, baking powder, and salt together; add in fourths to creamed mixture, mixing until blended after each addition. Chill dough thoroughly.
3. Roll a third of dough at a time ⅛ inch thick; cut with 2¼-inch round or fancy cutter. Transfer to ungreased cookie sheets.
4. Bake at 325°F 15 to 18 minutes.

*About 4½ dozen cookies*

*Note:* If desired, add sugar sparkle by evenly sprinkling *granulated sugar* over the rolled dough. Roll lightly to press sugar into dough. Or, add decorations by brushing rolled dough with slightly beaten *egg white* (or egg yolk beaten with 1 tablespoon water or milk); top with pieces of *angelica, citron,* or *candied cherries* or sprinkle with *colored sugar* or crushed *rock candy.*

*Brown Sugar Cookies:* Follow recipe for Lemon Sugar Cookies. Omit lemon peel and juice; add *1 teaspoon vanilla extract.* Substitute *1 cup firmly packed brown sugar* for granulated sugar.

# Gingerbread Men

| | |
|---|---|
| 4 ½ | **cups sifted all-purpose flour** |
| 1 | **tablespoon cinnamon** |
| 1 | **teaspoon salt** |
| 1 | **teaspoon baking soda** |
| 1 | **teaspoon ginger** |
| ½ | **teaspoon cloves** |
| ½ | **cup butter or margarine** |
| ½ | **cup firmly packed brown sugar** |
| 1 | **egg** |
| 1 | **cup molasses** |
| 2 | **teaspoons vinegar** |

1. Sift flour, cinnamon, salt, baking soda , ginger, and cloves together and set aside.
2. Cream butter or margarine until softened.
3. Add brown sugar gradually, creaming until light and fluffy after each addition.
4. Add egg and beat thoroughly.
5. Add molasses and vinegar gradually while beating.
6. Stir in dry ingredients.
7. Wrap dough in moisture-vaporproof material and chill in refrigerator 8 hrs. or overnight. Lightly grease cookie sheets.
8. Roll one portion of chilled dough at a time, ¼ in. thick, on lightly floured surface. Cut dough with gingerbread-man cookie cutter, or lay a cardboard pattern over dough and cut with sharp knife carefully around pattern. Using pancake turner, transfer cookies to cookie sheets.
9. Bake at 350°F about 10 minutes. When cool, add fancy decorations with frosting or candies.

*About 1½ doz. Gingerbread Men*
*or 2½ doz. round cookies*

# Poor Man's Cookies

| | |
|---|---|
| 5 | cups sifted all-purpose flour |
| 1 | teaspoon cardamom |
| 10 | egg yolks |
| 2 | egg whites |
| ¾ | cup sugar |
| 3 | tablespoons brandy |
| 1 | cup heavy cream |
| | Lard |

1. A deep saucepan or automatic deep fryer will be needed.
2. Sift flour and cardamom together and set aside.
3. Beat egg yolks, egg whites, sugar and brandy until mixture is thick and lemon-colored.
4. Add heavy cream slowly.
5. Blend in flour mixture, about ½ cup at a time, to make a soft dough. Wrap dough in waxed paper and chill overnight in refrigerator.
6. Set out a deep saucepan or automatic deep fryer and heat lard to 365°F to 370°F.
7. Meanwhile, roll dough, a small portion at a time, to ¹⁄₁₆-in. thickness on a lightly floured surface. Cut into diamond shapes, 5x2-in. (A pattern may be used as a guide around which to cut with a floured knife.) Make a lengthwise slit in the center of the diamond and pull one tip end through it and tuck back under itself.
8. Deep-fry only as many cookies at one time as will float uncrowded one layer deep in fat. Deep-fry 1 to 2 min., or until golden brown, turning once during deep-frying time. Drain over fat a few seconds before removing to absorbent paper. Sprinkle with confectioners' sugar.
9. Store in tightly covered containers.

*About 6 doz. cookies*

# Scottish Shortbread

| | |
|---|---|
| 2 | cups sifted all-purpose flour |
| 6 | tablespoons sugar |
| 2 | tablespoons cornstarch |
| ¾ | cup butter |

1. Sift flour, sugar, and cornstarch into a bowl. Cut in butter until mixture becomes a soft dough (requires working beyond the stage when particles are the size of rice kernels).
2. Shape dough into a ball; knead lightly with fingertips until mixture holds together.
3. Roll half of the dough at a time ¼ to ½ inch thick on a floured surface.
4. Cut into 1½x½-inch strips, or use fancy cutters. Place on ungreased cookie sheets.
5. Bake at 350°F 25 to 30 minutes; do not brown.

*2½ to 4 dozen cookies*

# Gingersnaps

| | |
|---|---|
| 1 | cup shortening |
| 1 | cup sugar |
| ⅔ | cup hot coffee |
| ⅔ | cup molasses |
| 5 | cups cake flour |
| 1 | teaspoon salt |
| 1 | teaspoon soda |
| 2 | teaspoons ginger |
| 1 | teaspoon cloves |
| 1 | teaspoon cinnamon |

1. Cream shortening and sugar thoroughly.
2. Add hot coffee to molasses and add to creamed mixture.
3. Sift dry ingredients together.
4. Add gradually to liquid mixture. Chill thoroughly.
5. Roll out on a pastry cloth ⅛ inch thick, cut out and bake in a moderate oven 350°F 17 minutes.

*14 dozen 2-inch cookies*

# Linzer Wreath Cookies

¼ cup (about 1 oz.) finely chopped walnuts
¼ cup sugar
2 cups sifted all-purpose flour
½ cup confectioners' sugar
¼ teaspoon baking soda
½ cup unsalted butter, chilled and cut in pieces
2 egg yolks, slightly beaten
¼ teaspoon vanilla extract
¼ teaspoon grated lemon peel
   Egg, slightly beaten
¼ cup thick jam, such as apricot or strawberry
2 tablespoons confectioners' sugar

1. Lightly grease cookie sheets.
2. Mix walnuts and sugar and set aside.
3. Sift flour, ½ cup confectioners' sugar and baking soda together into a large bowl.
4. Work butter into the dry ingredients by pressing against bottom and sides of bowl with a fork.
5. Gradually add to the ingredients in the bowl, mixing with a fork after each addition, a mixture of egg yolks, vanilla extract and lemon peel. (Mixture will be crumbly.) Gather dough into a ball. Turn dough out onto lightly floured surface. Work with hands, squeezing dough until well blended. Shape into smooth ball with palms of hands. If dough becomes too soft, chill slightly in refrigerator.
6. Roll dough ⅛ to ¼ in. thick. With lightly floured 2-in. scalloped cookie cutter, cut dough into rounds. Place one half of the rounds onto cookie sheets. Using a thimble dipped in flour, cut ½-in. holes in centers of remaining rounds, forming rings. Brush all the rounds and rings with egg.
7. Dip top surface of rings into the nut-sugar mixture. Place rings, coated-side up, on cookie sheets (not on top of cookie rounds).
8. Bake at 350°F 15 to 20 min., or until lightly browned. Remove cookies to cooling racks.
9. Set out jam. Spread ½ to ¾ teaspoon of the jam onto each plain cookie round. Top each with a nut-topped cookie ring. Sprinkle confectioner's sugar onto cookies.

*About 1½ doz. cookies*

# Danish Christmas Crullers

5 egg yolks
1 egg
1 cup sugar
5 teaspoons finely shredded lemon peel
3¾ cups sifted all-purpose flour
½ cup heavy cream
   Lard for deep frying

1. Combine egg yolks, egg, sugar, and lemon peel. Beat until very thick. Beating only until smooth after each addition, alternately add flour in thirds and cream in halves. Chill thoroughly.
2. About 20 minutes before ready to deep fry, start heating lard to 365°F.
3. Working with a small amount of dough at a time (keep remainder of dough chilled) on a floured surface, knead dough until smooth and roll it out thin. Cut into 3x1½-inch strips, slanting the ends. Cut a slit about 1½ inches long in center of each strip and draw one end through the slit.
4. Fry in the hot fat until golden brown, turning once.
5. Remove to absorbent paper and drain thoroughly before serving or storing.

*8 to 12 cookies*
*(depending on thickness)*

*Danish Christmas Crullers II:* Follow recipe for Danish Christmas Crullers I. Omit lemon peel and blend **½ to 1 teaspoon ground cardamom** with the flour.

# Crown Jewels

Topping, (below)
1 cup butter or margarine
½ teaspoon grated orange peel
½ cup sugar
2 hard-cooked egg yolks, sieved
2 cups sifted all-purpose flour

1. Prepare Topping.
2. Cream butter with orange peel. Gradually add sugar, beating until fluffy.
3. Blend in sieved hard-cooked egg yolks. Add flour in fourths, mixing well after each addition.
4. Press dough firmly onto bottom of ungreased 15x10x1-inch jelly roll pan.
5. Bake at 350°F 20 minutes.
6. While still warm, spread with Date Topping and then Candied Fruit Topping. Cool thoroughly and cut into fancy shapes.

*About 3 dozen cookies*

# Candied Fruit Topping

½ lb. red and green candied pineapple, finely chopped (1⅔ cups)
¼ lb. candied red cherries, finely chopped (⅔ cup)
2 oz. candied orange peel, finely chopped (⅓ cup)
⅓ cup rum

1. Mix candied fruit with rum in the top of a double boiler.
2. Heat, covered, over simmering water 30 minutes, stirring occasionally; cool slightly.

# Date Topping

1. Mix *1 cup (about 7 ounces) pitted dates,* finely chopped, with *¼ cup orange juice* in the top of a double boiler.
2. Heat, covered, over simmering water 10 minutes, stirring occasionally; cool.

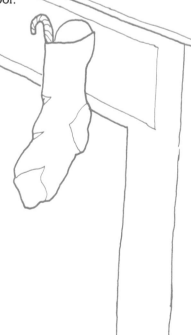

# Snowy Icing

1 **cup sugar**
¼ **cup water**
**Few grains salt**
1 **egg white**
1 **teaspoon vanilla extract**

1. Mix the sugar, water, and salt in a small saucepan; stir over low heat until sugar is dissolved.
2. Cook without stirring until mixture spins a 2-inch thread (about 230°F) when a small amount is dropped from a spoon.
3. Beat egg white until stiff, not dry, peaks are formed. Continue beating egg white while pouring hot syrup over it in a steady thin stream. After all the syrup is added, continue beating until icing is very thick and forms rounded peaks (holds shape).
4. Blend in extract.

*About 2½ cups icing*

# Fruity Polish Mazurek

2 **cups sifted all-purpose flour**
1 **cup sugar**
½ **teaspoon salt**
½ **cup butter or margarine**
1 **egg**
¼ **cup half-and-half**
1⅔ **cups seedless raisins, chopped**
1½ **cups pitted dates, chopped**
1¼ **cups dried figs, chopped**
1 **cup chopped walnuts**
⅓ **cup sugar**
2 **eggs**
½ **cup orange juice**
3 **tablespoons lemon juice**

1. Sift flour, 1 cup sugar, and salt together into a bowl. Cut in butter.
2. Beat egg and cream together and add to flour mixture. Mix lightly with a fork until mixture forms a ball.
3. Spread dough in a greased 15x10x1-inch jelly roll pan.
4. Bake at 350°F about 30 minutes, or until dough is lightly browned around edges.
5. Meanwhile, prepare fruit topping by combining the chopped fruits and walnuts with a mixture of the ⅓ cup sugar, 2 eggs, and fruit juices; mix thoroughly. Spread over partially baked dough in pan.
6. Return to oven and bake 20 minutes.
7. Remove to wire rack; cool. If desired, garnish with **candied fruit** such as candied cherries, candied pineapple, and/or candied orange peel. Cut in 2x1-inch pieces.

*About 6 dozen cookies*

# Desserts

# Nesselrode Pudding

| | |
|---|---|
| 1½ | doz. single ladyfingers (or use sponge cake cut in 4x¾x½-in. pieces) |
| 2 | egg yolks |
| ½ | cup sugar |
| ¼ | cup (2 oz.) sherry |
| 1¾ | cups chilled heavy cream (beat only one half at a time) |
| ⅓ | cup confectioners' sugar |
| 1¼ | teaspoons vanilla extract |
| 2 | egg whites |
| ⅛ | teaspoon salt |
| 1 | jar (10 oz.) Nesselrode mixture (about 1¼ cups) |

1. Set out a 9x5x3-in. loaf pan. Put a medium-size bowl and a rotary beater into refrigerator to chill.
2. Set out ladyfingers. Line sides of the loaf pan with the ladyfingers and set aside.
3. Put egg yolks into a large bowl and beat until very thick and lemon-colored.
4. Add sugar gradually, beating well after each addition.
5. Add sherry gradually, beating constantly.
6. Set egg yolk mixture aside.
7. Using the chilled bowl and beater, beat heavy cream until cream is of medium consistency (piles softly).
8. Beat confectioners' sugar and vanilla extract into whipped cream with a few final strokes. Set in refrigerator while beating egg whites.
9. Using clean beater, beat egg whites and salt until stiff, not dry, peaks are formed.
10. Blend Nesselrode mixture into the egg yolk mixture.
11. Spread the whipped cream and egg whites over the egg yolk mixture and gently fold together. Turn mixture into the prepared pan and spread evenly.
12. Freeze until firm, about 12 hrs.

*About 8 servings*

*Note:* If desired, omit ladyfingers and freeze mixture in refrigerator trays.

# Frozen Christmas Pudding

| | |
|---|---|
| 1½ | cups macaroon crumbs (about 14 small macaroons, crushed) |
| ½ | cup chopped pecans |
| ½ | cup chopped pitted dates |
| ¼ | cup chopped candied pineapple |
| ¼ | cup chopped candied orange peel |
| 1¼ | teaspoons grated lemon peel |
| ¼ | teaspoon ground cinnamon |
| ¼ | teaspoon ground nutmeg |
| 8 | marshmallows, quartered |
| ¼ | cup orange juice |
| ¼ | cup sugar |
| 1 | cup heavy cream, whipped |

1. Combine crumbs, pecans, dates, pineapple, orange and lemon peels, cinnamon, and nutmeg in a bowl; set aside.
2. Heat marshmallows, orange juice, and sugar together in the top of a double boiler over boiling water until marshmallows are melted, stirring occasionally. Blend into fruit mixture. Fold in whipped cream.
3. Put 10 paper baking cups, 2¼x1¼ inches, into refrigerator trays or muffin-pan wells. Spoon mixture into cups; freeze until firm.
4. When ready to serve, garnish each with a holly spray formed with red cinnamon candies and pieces of green gumdrops.

*10 servings*

*Note:* If macaroons are moist, dry and toast them slightly in a 325°F oven before crushing.

# Molded Holiday Pudding

| | |
|---|---|
| 3 | cups boiling water |
| 1¼ | cups prunes |
| 1 | cup dried apricots |
| 1 | cup sugar |
| 1 | teaspoon ground cinnamon |
| 1 | teaspoon ground nutmeg |
| 1 | teaspoon ground allspice |
| 1¼ | cups orange juice |
| 3 | env. unflavored gelatin |
| 1½ | cups golden raisins, plumped |
| 2¼ | cups candied cherries |
| ⅓ | cup diced candied citron |
| ⅓ | cup diced candied lemon peel |
| 1½ | cups walnuts, coarsely chopped |
| 3 | env. (2 oz. each) dessert topping mix, or 3 cups heavy cream, whipped |

1. Pour boiling water over prunes and apricots in a saucepan. Return to boiling, cover, and simmer about 45 minutes, or until fruit is tender. Drain and reserve 1 cup liquid. Set liquid aside until cold. Remove and discard prune pits.
2. Force prunes and apricots through food mill or sieve into a large bowl. Stir in a mixture of the sugar, cinnamon, nutmeg, and allspice, mixing until sugar is dissolved. Blend in the orange juice and mix thoroughly.
3. Soften gelatin in the 1 cup reserved liquid in a small saucepan. Stir over low heat until gelatin is dissolved. Stir into fruit-spice mixture. Chill until mixture is slightly thickened, stirring occasionally.
4. Blend raisins, cherries, citron, lemon peel, and walnuts into gelatin mixture.
5. Prepare the dessert topping according to package directions, or whip the cream. Gently fold into fruit mixture, blending thoroughly. Turn into 9- or 10-inch tubed pan. Chill until firm.
6. Unmold onto chilled serving plate.

*20 to 24 servings*

*Note:* If a less sweet pudding is desired, decrease sugar to ½ cup. To develop flavor of dessert, prepare 2 to 4 days in advance of serving.

# New Orleans Holiday Pudding

| | |
|---|---|
| 1½ | pts. heavy cream |
| 5 | cups water |
| 1¼ | cups (about ½ lb.) prunes |
| 1 | cup (about 6 oz.) dried apricots |
| 1½ | cups (about 7½ oz.) golden raisins |
| 1 | lb. (about 2¼ cups) candied cherries |
| ⅓ | cup (about 2 oz.) diced candied citron |
| ⅓ | cup (about 2 oz.) diced candied lemon peel |
| 1 | cup sugar |
| 1 | teaspoon cinnamon |
| 1 | teaspoon nutmeg |
| 1 | teaspoon allspice |
| 1 | cup orange juice |
| 3 | tablespoons brandy |
| 1½ | cups (about 6 oz.) walnuts |
| 1½ | cups cold reserved prune-apricot liquid |
| 3 | env. unflavored gelatin |

1. Set out a 9- or 10-in. tubed pan and a 3-qt. saucepan with a cover.
2. Chill in refrigerator a bowl, rotary beater and heavy cream.
3. Meanwhile, pour 3 cups water into the saucepan.
4. Add prunes and apricots to the water. Bring to boiling; cover and simmer about 20 min., or until fruit is tender.
5. Bring 2 cups water to boiling in a small saucepan.
6. Add raisins and bring water again to boiling.
7. Drain raisins and put into a large bowl with cherries, citron, and lemon peel. Set fruit mixture aside.
8. Turn prune-apricot mixture into colander or large sieve to drain. Reserve liquid in a measuring cup (add water if needed to yield 1½ cups liquid); set aside to cool. Pit prunes.
9. Force prune-apricot mixture through sieve or food mill into the saucepan to make a puree. Stir in a mixture of sugar, cinnamon, nutmeg and allspice until sugar is dissolved.
10. Blend into candied fruit mixture with orange juice and brandy. Cover and set aside for about 1½ hrs., stirring occasionally.
11. Coarsely chop walnuts and set aside.
12. Pour reserved prune-apricot liquid into a heavy saucepan. Sprinkle gelatin evenly over liquid.
13. Set saucepan over low heat and stir constantly until gelatin is completely dissolved. Blend the dissolved gelatin into the fruit mixture. Mix in the chopped walnuts. Set mixture in refrigerator while whipping cream.
14. Pour one third of chilled heavy cream into the chilled bowl. Beat with the chilled rotary beater until cream is of medium consistency (piles softly). Turn whipped cream onto fruit-gelatin mixture.
15. Beat remaining heavy cream as above and turn onto previously whipped cream. Gently fold together, blending thoroughly. Carefully spoon into prepared pan. Chill in refrigerator until firm. Unmold onto a large serving plate.
16. This dessert will keep for several days in the refrigerator.

*20 to 24 servings, depending upon size of tubed pan*

*For Festive Topping* — Cover bottom of pan with chopped nuts. Reserve 12 cherries and arrange in clusters of three, moving nuts to let cherries touch bottom of pan. When spooning mixture over nuts and cherries, gently press mixture over nuts to cover entirely.

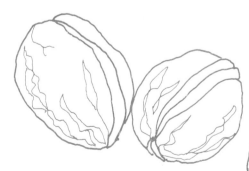

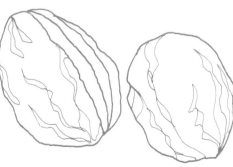

# Marzipan (Marcepan)

1   **pound blanched almonds**
1   **pound confectioners' sugar**
2   **tablespoons orange water or rose water**
    **Food coloring**
    **Decorations (colored sugar, dragees, or chocolate shot)**

1. Grind almonds very fine. Combine in a saucepan with sugar and flavoring. Cook until mixture leaves side of pan.
2. Roll almond mixture on flat surface to ½-inch thickness. Cut out small heart shapes. Or, shape into small fruits or vegetables.
3. Paint with appropriate food coloring or coat as desired, for example, with red sugar for "strawberries" and cocoa for "potatoes." Decorate with dragees or chocolate shot. Place on waxed paper to dry 2 hours.

*2 pounds*

# Rich Chocolate Pudding

2   **ounces (2 squares) unsweetened chocolate**
2   **cups milk**
½   **cup sugar**
2   **tablespoons cornstarch**
¼   **teaspoon salt**
2   **teaspoons vanilla extract**
2   **teaspoons butter or margarine**

1. Put chocolate and milk into the top of a double boiler. Cook over simmering water until chocolate is melted, stirring occasionally.
2. Combine sugar, cornstarch, and salt; gradually add to chocolate mixture, stirring constantly.
3. Cook and stir over boiling water until thickened. Remove from heat; stir in vanilla extract and butter. Pour into serving dishes and chill.
4. Serve with **whipped cream** or **whipped dessert topping**.

*About 4 servings*

# Double-Boiler Chocolate Souffle

1   **cup milk**
2   **ounces (2 squares) unsweetened chocolate**
3   **tablespoons butter or margarine**
3   **tablespoons flour**
½   **cup sugar**
4   **egg yolks**
1   **teaspoon vanilla extract**
4   **egg whites**
¼   **teaspoon cream of tartar**

1. Combine milk and chocolate in a saucepan; cook over low heat, stirring occasionally, until chocolate is melted and mixture is blended.
2. Meanwhile, melt butter in saucepan; stir in the flour and cook until mixture is bubbly. Remove from heat and stir in the milk-chocolate mixture; blend in the sugar. Return to heat and bring the mixture to boiling, stirring constantly.
3. Beat egg yolks until very thick. Adding gradually, beat chocolate mixture into egg yolks until thoroughly blended. Mix in vanilla extract. Cool to lukewarm.
4. Beat egg whites until frothy; add cream of tartar and continue beating until stiff, not dry, peaks are formed. Gently fold in the chocolate mixture until thoroughly blended.
5. Butter inside of top section of a 2-quart metal double boiler; turn mixture into it. Cover and set over boiling water (water should rise to no more than one half of the height of double-boiler top).
6. Keeping water gently boiling, cook 60 to 70 minutes, or until a metal knife inserted halfway between center and edge of souffle comes out clean.
7. Run a spatula around edge of souffle and invert onto a serving plate, or spoon into individual serving dishes. Serve immediately; garnish with **sweetened whipped cream**.

*About 6 servings*

# Trifle

|       |                                    |
|-------|------------------------------------|
|       | **Pound cake**                     |
| ½     | **cup brandy or rum**              |
| ¼     | **cup sugar**                      |
| 1     | **envelope unflavored gelatin**    |
| ⅛     | **teaspoon salt**                  |
| 5     | **egg yolks**                      |
| 1¾    | **cups milk**                      |
| 1     | **teaspoon vanilla extract**       |
| 3     | **egg whites**                     |
| ¼     | **cup sugar**                      |
| ¼     | **cup chilled whipping cream, whipped** |

1. Cut pound cake into 1-inch pieces. Arrange in a layer over bottom of a 2-quart shallow casserole. Pour brandy over cake pieces. Set aside.
2. Combine ¼ cup sugar, gelatin, and salt in the top of a double boiler; blend thoroughly. Beat egg yolks with milk in a bowl until thoroughly blended. Combine with the gelatin mixture in top of double boiler.
3. Set over boiling water and cook, stirring occasionally about 5 minutes, or until the gelatin is completely dissolved. Remove from heat and stir in vanilla extract. Chill until mixture mounds slightly when dropped from a spoon; stir occasionally.
4. Beat the egg whites until frothy. Add ¼ cup sugar gradually, beating thoroughly after each addition. Continue to beat until stiff peaks are formed.
5. Spread egg whites and whipped cream over gelatin mixture and gently fold together. Turn into casserole. Chill until firm.
6. When ready to serve, garnish with **candied cherries, slivered almonds,** and **pieces of angelica.** If desired, garnish with a border of sweetened whipped cream forced through a pastry bag and star decorating tube.

*About 12 servings*

# Creme Brulee

|    |                                      |
|----|--------------------------------------|
| 4  | **egg yolks, slightly beaten**       |
| ¼  | **cup sugar**                        |
| 2  | **cups whipping cream, scalded**     |
| 2  | **teaspoons vanilla extract**        |
| ½  | **cup firmly packed brown sugar**    |

1. Combine egg yolks with sugar; blend thoroughly. Gradually add hot cream, stirring until sugar is dissolved. Strain into a 1-quart baking dish.
2. Blend in vanilla extract. Place baking dish in a shallow pan with hot water and bake at 325°F 50 minutes, or until a knife inserted in custard comes out clean.
3. Remove from oven and set baking dish on wire rack to cool; chill thoroughly.
4. Before serving, sift brown sugar evenly over top. Place under broiler with top a least 5 inches from heat; broil until sugar is melted. Watch carefully so sugar will not burn.
5. Cool and refrigerate until ready to serve.

*About 6 servings*

# Sesame Seed Candy (Pasteli)

|    |                            |
|----|----------------------------|
| ½  | **cup honey**              |
| 2  | **cups sugar**             |
| ½  | **cup water**              |
| 3  | **cups sesame seed, toasted** |

1. Blend honey, sugar, and water in a heavy skillet. Cook over low heat, stirring frequently. Bring to a firm ball state, 250°F on a candy thermometer (syrup will be a light gold color). Stir in sesame seed.
2. Spread in a buttered 12x8x1½-inch pan. Break into pieces.

*2 to 3 dozen pieces depending on size*

# Fruit-Nut Candy Squares

| | |
|---|---|
| 1 | cup (about ⅓ lb.) dried figs |
| 1 | cup (about 6 oz.) pitted dates |
| 1 | cup (about ⅓ lb.) dried apricots |
| ½ | cup (about 2 oz.) nuts |
| ½ | cup moist flaked coconut |
| 2 | teaspoons grated orange peel |
| 3 | tablespoons orange juice |
| ½ | teaspoon cinnamon |
| | Confectioners' sugar |

1. Lightly grease an 8-in. square pan.
2. Rinse figs, dates and apricots and put through coarse blade of food chopper.
3. Coarsely chop nuts.
4. Combine fruits and nuts with coconut and a mixture of orange peel, orange juice and cinnamon.
5. Mix well. Turn into pan and press evenly over bottom. Chill well in refrigerator.
6. Sprinkle with confectioners' sugar.
7. Cut into 1-in. squares. Remove with flexible spatula.

*64 squares*

# Snowballs Adrift

| | |
|---|---|
| 1 | cup moist shredded coconut |
| 1 | qt. ice cream |

1. Ice cream of any desired flavor may be used for snowballs. It must be firm before shaping balls.
2. Spread coconut in a chilled shallow pan.
3. With a scoop, rinsed each time in hot water, quickly form 6 to 8 balls of ice cream.
4. After forming each ball, roll immediately in the coconut. Place snowballs in chilled refrigerator tray and cover with waxed paper. Before serving, spoon chocolate syrup into individual dishes and in each one float a snowball.

*6 to 8 servings*

# Kicki's Best Caramels

| | |
|---|---|
| 1 | cup heavy cream |
| 2 | cups sugar |
| 3 | oz. brown sugar |
| 3 | oz. molasses |
| 3 | oz. unsweetened cocoa |

1. In a heavy saucepan mix all ingredients. Bring mixture to a boil while stirring with a wooden spoon. Simmer for 20 minutes stirring occassionally. Test when a drop of the mixture sets in cold water the mixture is ready. The drop should be easy to form into a ball.
2. Pour the mixture into a greased baking pan and let it stand for a while. Cut the mixture into squares before it has set and wrap in greaseproof paper.

# Christmas Candy Balls

| | |
|---|---|
| 2 | medium potatoes, scrubbed (do not pare) |
| 1 | cup sugar |
| 1 | teaspoon vanilla extract |
| 2 | cups chopped pecans |
| 1 | cup confectioners' sugar |
| 1 | teaspoon ground cinnamon |
| | Candied red or green cherries, cut in halves |

1. Cook potatoes in their skins, peel, press through ricer or food mill. Mix in sugar, vanilla extract, and nuts. Chill.
2. Form little balls; coat them with confectioners' sugar mixed with cinnamon. Put into small fluted paper cups and garnish with cherry halves.
3. Store in refrigerator until ready to serve.

*About 2 dozen balls*

# Cream Puff or Choux Paste

1    cup hot water
½    cup butter
1    tablespoon sugar
½    teaspoon salt
1    cup all-purpose flour
4    eggs

1. Put hot water, butter, sugar, and salt into a saucepan and bring to a rolling boil.
2. Add the flour all at one time. Beat vigorously with a wooden spoon until mixture leaves sides of pan and forms a smooth ball. Remove from heat.
3. Add eggs, one at a time, beating until smooth after each addition. Continue beating until mixture is thick and smooth.
4. Dough may be shaped and baked at once, or wrapped in waxed paper and stored in refrigerator overnight.
5. Complete as directed in the following variation.

*1 Dozen Large or 4 Dozen Miniature Puffs or Eclairs*

*Cream Puff Christmas Tree:* Prepare recipe for Cream Puff or Choux Paste. Force dough through a pastry bag and tube, or drop by spoonfuls 2 inches apart onto lightly greased baking sheets. Bake at 425°F 20 minutes, or until golden brown. Turn off oven. Prick puffs with a fork and return to oven for 20 minutes. Remove puffs to wire racks and cool completely. Cut off tops of puffs. Spoon about 3 tablespoons *Eggnog Pineapple Filling (below)*, into each shell. Replace tops. On a serving plate. arrange puffs to form a tree.

*18 to 24 Cream Puffs*

# Eggnog Pineapple Filling

1½    tablespoons cornstarch
2    tablespoons cold water
3    cups dairy eggnog
½    teaspoon vanilla extract
1    can (8½ oz.) crushed pineapple, well drained
1    cup quartered maraschino cherries
¼    cup flaked coconut

1. Mix a blend of the cornstarch and water and eggnog in a heavy saucepan. Stirring constantly, bring rapidly to boiling. Cook and stir 2 to 3 minutes. Remove from heat.
2. Immediately turn into a chilled bowl; do not scrape pan. Mix in remaining ingredients. Cool over ice and water, stirring occasionally. Use to fill cream puffs.

*About 3½ cups filling*

# Beverages

## Egg Nog

| | |
|---|---|
| **1** | **egg, beaten** |
| **1** | **tablespoon sugar or honey** |
| | **Salt** |
| **¾** | **cup milk** |
| **¼** | **teaspoon vanilla** |
| | **Dash nutmeg** |

1. Combine egg with sugar and salt, add milk and vanilla.
2. Serve cold in tall glasses and sprinkle with nutmeg.
3. For a fluffy eggnog separate egg, beat white until stiff, then fold into egg yolk mixture.
4. May be served hot or cold, for 1.

## Wassail

| | |
|---|---|
| **3** | **cups water** |
| **½** | **cup orange juice** |
| **¼** | **cup lemon juice** |
| **3** | **whole oranges, studded with cloves (see Note)** |
| **1½** | **teaspoons whole allspice** |
| **2** | **sticks cinnamon** |
| **¼** | **teaspoon nutmeg** |
| **¼** | **teaspoon ginger** |
| **2** | **cups water** |
| **¾** | **cup sugar** |
| **¼** | **cup instant tea** |
| **½** | **gallon apple cider** |

1. Combine 3 cups water, orange juice, lemon juice, 1 studded orange, and spices in an electric cooker.
2. Cover and cook on Low 2½ hours.
3. Bake the remaining studded oranges in a 350°F oven 45 minutes; reserve until serving time.
4. Meanwhile, stir 2 cups water into sugar in a saucepan; bring to boiling, stirring only until sugar dissolves, and boil 5 minutes.
5. Add sugar syrup, instant tea, and apple cider to spiced fruit juice mixture in electric cooker.
6. Cover and cook on Low 15 to 30 minutes, or until heated through.
7. Strain, transfer to punch bowl, pierce baked oranges several times with wooden pick, float them in wassail, and serve in punch cups. Make sure that bowl and punch cups are heatproof.

*About 3½ quarts punch*

*Note:* To stud oranges, pierce with wooden pick at 1-inch intervals and insert cloves.

# Champagne Bowl

| | |
|---|---|
| **1** | **bottle Champagne, Canary wine or other sparkling wine** |
| **1** | **bottle club soda** |
| **3** | **oz. maraschino or curacao liqueur** |
| **1** | **finely sliced lemon ice cubes** |

1. Mix wine, club soda and liqueur. Add ice cubes, lemon slices and serve.

*Serves 6*

# Cranberry Punch

| | |
|---|---|
| **4** | **cups firm cranberries, rinsed** |
| **4** | **cups water** |
| **1½** | **cups sugar** |
| **2** | **tablespoons lemon juice** |
| **4** | **cups pineapple juice, chilled** |
| **1** | **cup orange juice, chilled** |

1. Combine cranberries and water in a saucepan. Cook over medium heat until cranberry skins pop.
2. Sieve cooked cranberries. Stir in sugar and lemon juice. Return to saucepan; bring to boiling and cook 2 minutes, stirring constantly. Immediately remove from heat; cool and chill thoroughly in refrigerator.
3. To serve, pour over ice cubes in a large pitcher or punch bowl. Stir in pineapple and orange juices. Serve in punch cups.

*About 1½ Quarts Punch*

*Note:* For a refreshing start to a luncheon or dinner, fill small glasses with Cranberry Punch and top each glass with a small scoop of *lemon sherbet*.

# Sage Cider Punch

| | |
|---|---|
| | **"Sage brew"** * |
| | **"Tea brew"** ** |
| **1** | **qt. apple cider** |
| **1** | **cup sugar** |
| **2** | **tablespoons lime juice (1 small lime)** |

1. Prepare the sage and tea brews; set aside.
2. Meanwhile, combine cider and sugar in a saucepan; set over low heat and stir until sugar is dissolved. Cover saucepan and heat the cider to simmering.
3. Add the strained sage and tea brews and the lime juice; blend thoroughly. Cover and keep hot over low heat until ready to serve. (Do not boil.)
4. Serve in small glasses or mugs. If desired, float several *sage leaves* on each serving.

*About 5½ cups Punch*

*To prepare "sage brew," pour *1 cup boiling water* over *2 tablespoons leaf sage* in a small saucepan. Bring to simmering; cover tightly and remove from heat. Let stand about 10 minutes to brew. Strain through cheesecloth or a fine sieve.

*About ⅔ cup*

**To prepare "tea brew," pour 1 cup boiling water over *1 tea bag* in a small saucepan; cover tightly and let stand about 10 minutes. Remove tea bag.

*About 1 cup*

# Index